Preparing for the New Jerusalem

Seeing the Light at Last

Carol L. Briggs

authorHOUSE®

AuthorHouse™
1663 Liberty Drive
Bloomington, IN 47403
www.authorhouse.com
Phone: 1-800-839-8640

First published by AuthorHouse 5/9/2011

ISBN: 978-1-4567-1483-3 (sc)
ISBN: 978-1-4567-1482-6 (e)

Library of Congress Control Number: 2010918645

Printed in the United States of America
Library of Congress Control Number: 2010918645
*Any people depicted in stock imagery provided by Thinkstock are
models,*
and such images are being used for illustrative purposes only.
Certain stock imagery © Thinkstock.

This book is printed on acid-free paper.

A PERSONAL NOTE TO YOU, THE READER:

A Pastor at church one Sunday morning made the statement during his sermon, "God told me to change the subject of my sermon this morning."

A grumbling noise came from my husband, Jack, who was sitting beside me. Later, when I asked him what he was grumbling about, he answered, "I don't trust anyone who says, 'God told me to do this' as if they have a direct pipeline to Almighty God!" (This was 27 years ago).

Being a relatively new attendee of a Bible-preaching, Jesus-praising, unashamed worshiping-God kind of church, Jack's words had an influence on my recently-discovered passion for Jesus Christ, our Savior and Lord. Those words set me back a couple of paces in my "stepping out in Faith" walk with the Lord, our Lord.

However, the more I hesitantly prayed out loud (it was very difficult for me to unselfconsciously show my feelings—especially in front of others), read scripture, and talked to Jesus during my quiet time...the more I disagreed with what Jack said.

The more I walked in the Lord's will, the more I felt His communication with me; and, after attending a Bible Study, EXPERIENCING GOD, found the different ways He lets us know the choices and decisions we need to make to stay in His will. The Comforter, the Holy Spirit, (when you accept Jesus as your personal Savior) will be your guide and will help you discern what Jesus wants you to do. He uses other Christians, Scripture, listening to the Word, and perhaps eventually a still small voice in your mind, or in some cases, a loud whisper of urgency.[1]Don't let anyone make you doubt that you can talk with God (Jesus). When you are in His will, and even though you may not have come to the point of complete surrender to Him, He will commune with you...not always in words; however, doors open that were not open before you prayed; or, perhaps doors slam shut to keep you from making a wrong decision. (Be careful, though, the "father of lies" is very good at disguising himself to look like and sound like our Savior).

As soon as I internalized the realization that God is in control of everything...even small trivial things, my thinking changed, and I began to turn my life over to Him. It is not easy to relinquish control when all those years my goal was to"control my own destiny," a motto straight from the bag of tricks of the Deceiver.

This book is for people like me...calling myself a Christian but not even realizing that to be aChristian, one has to have a personal relationship with Christ. Professing before men that He is your Savior is just the beginning. He will impact your life every day in every way if you are willing to pray and ask Him to use you. Let Him know that you are available for whatever He shows you is His will. Praise Him and thank Him whenever He blesses you, which is all day long when you see the joy and peace you have--in contrast to the worry and fear you had before you found Jesus! (There will still be times when you have worry and fear, but when you remember to turn the problem over to Him, it will not look hopeless as it did before Jesus.)

I have usedmany different fonts—bold for Bible verses, italics for my musing thoughts...regular print for auto-biographical writing. My periods of ellipsis are prominent throughout the book. Some of my sentences ramble on and on, which makesthe story more realistic. *He has been so close to me and in me during this writing...as if He is reading over my shoulder, putting thoughts into my mind, and proofreading the finished work.*

In this book, I am attempting to lay out for you, the reader, happenings I remember that indicate to me the Holy Spirit was gently nudging me toward the day of His revealing... when He opened my eyes to the "New Jerusalem" (which begins when you make Him your King over you here on this earth).

Oh, beloved, read this book with an open heart and look back on your life and see where He is leading you to a complete emptying of "self" and a complete filling of our "Triune" God who will satisfy your every need and make your life rich and fulfilling...*while you are telling others HOW He is renewing you.*

Maybe you can relate to some of the trials my brothers and I had to experience before we woke up to what our Creator really wants for us. It is very difficult to discern what is truth and what is the world's "Hype" (Satan's smokescreen). *Only Jesus can make it clear for you.*

One more thing...I'm hoping many different walks of life will read this book and get its simple message...if you become irritated when I put another meaning of the word in parenthesis to explain more clearly, please be patient... God made me a teacher. He wouldn't let me write a book just for people who read many books...but also for those who rarely read the Bible, or any book, either because of a limited vocabulary, a disability, or a lack of experience in spiritual matters, who need to know the Savior is there for them; and might read this book (or someone might read it to them) out of desperation because their trials (without Jesus) might have led them to complete despair--those who might need to cry out to Jesus to come to them before it is too late.(and don't even realize He is there for them.)

He wants you to know how much He loves you and if you will only ask, He will come to you and be a better Friend than any other.

Read how Jonathan found his best friend...*"Some weeks before his thirteenth birthday, having just witnessed a remarkable change in his elder sister who had 'gotten saved and gone religious,' Jonathan entered his bedroom one afternoon. Sitting down on the bed – no formula, no religious posture, no prayers – Jonathan said simply, forthrightly, 'God, if You're real, I really want to know You.' What transpired both startled him and filled him with awe. Suddenly, the room began to fill with bright light, so bright that it was white. The light was as real as to be almost tangible. Aghast, but not afraid, Jonathan opened his mouth in amazement. It was awesome. As he sat transfixed with mouth agape, the light moved toward him like a swirling mist. It entered his open mouth and descended into his deepest belly. He felt the warmth as it went down. When it had settled in his belly he felt a peace and joy he'd never known before...and more, much more than anything, he knew that he knew JESUS.*

Jesus is God and He had come in response to a young boy's sincere cry. There had been no church, no preacher, no Bible, only the cry of a lost soul searching for TRUTH and the TRUTH had revealed Himself. What a God! What a salvation!" from[1]RECKLESSLY ABANDONED by Michael Howard.

He's waiting for you to turn over every burden you are carrying needlessly...HE WILL SET YOU FREE!

[2]John 8:31) To the Jews who had believed Him, Jesus said, "If you hold to My teaching, you are really My disciples. 32) Then you will know the truth, and the truth will set you free."

My freedom began back in 1981, when Pastor Hinckley gave the invitation, and the white knuckles on my hands grasping the pew before me gave way to the urge to walk up that aisle and let everyone know that His conviction in my heart wasto surrender to Jesus and let Him be the ONLY Lord of my Life. Even though the Holy Spirit had been with me for many years, I had resisted complete surrender in some areas--thereby the bad decisions and the trials that resulted. When I realized my two teen-aged daughters, Ursula and Katrina, were right along beside me, at first I had some thoughts that maybe they weren't aware of the significance of what they were doing; however, my joy over-ruled those thoughts, *because Jesus would handle that. I know now that once anyone acknowledges their choice is Jesus, He will take it from there! (Just do it!)*

Pastor Hinckley explained to us that Baptism is not necessary for our salvation; because, once we are saved, we are "born again" and baptized in the Spirit; however, our desire to please our Savior compels us to follow His example and have our "old" self washed away and be resurrected in Jesus as a symbol to others that we belong to Jesus.

Not having a Baptismal pool in our little church, the Saubles offered their new cattle tank just installed on top of a hill in one of their winter pastures. Jesus was there on top of that hill, where we could see His handicraft for miles around. When Pastor Hinckley dunked each one of the three of us in that pure, sparkling well-water--pumped there by an old-fashioned windmill--in their minds, every church member on that hill was renewing their baptismal experience and singing "Shall We Gather at the River." Mind-boggling!

Thus began my truly spiritual "Walk" with Jesus...He was taking each "scale" off as I could handle it, as all those years of "self-aggrandizement" (taking credit for everything instead of giving the glory to God) had left many flakes of plaque on my thinking. He is showing me how to develop the "mindset of Jesus"...and will continue in this task until the New Jerusalem!

Writing this book has been a "Dangerous Adventure," as my then three-year old Granddaughter, Madelaine, said to her Grandpa, as he lifted her down from Patches, the Paint horse Jack had given to me when we were married. "A dangerous adventure" for her because the horse was so big and scary, and, she had actually sat on this huge back by herself—without Momma. A "dangerous adventure" for me because writing a book about the most important subject in the world—access to eternal life with Jesus-- is such a big and scary task for me; but, **nothing is**

impossible with God. Luke 1:37. I know now why our Pastor David has mentioned several times, "It is an awesome responsibility to teach my flock God's Word. Much prayer and study by ALLis necessary to get it God's Way." (Pastor David Downs is truly a preacher/teacher anointed by God.)

If only one person wakes up because of reading this book, it will be a "fulfillment of my purpose" —because our Heavenly Shepherd doesn't want to lose even "one lamb."

Prologue:

When I look back over my life, I can see how Jesus has been with me FROM THE TIME OF CONCEPTION...never had it entered my mind until recently that God had orchestrated my entire life to lead up 'til now when I am finally sincerely loving and praising Him for it. He was "PREPARING me FOR THE NEW JERUSALEM" before I was born! Awesome... light bulb beaming above my head! Have you ever thought of it that way?

I ask myself, "How could I have been oblivious to what has been here 'before my nose' for these many years?" Oh, yes, I spouted, "They've been given a gift of God!" when my friends would have babies...or, "God's little bundle of joy!" That was in my conscious mind; but never penetrated deeply enough to realize He even designed the sperm which fertilized (the egg) us new little humans (in His image, I might add). He knew me and loved me before (my) time...Wow!

How sad when some are led astray by the evil "deceiver" and never realize God's purpose for their life...who never see deeply enough to hear God's voice, or read His Word enough to wake up from their slumbering, bumbling walk through this world of pitfalls.

How sad when Satan is able to invade and set up a smoke screen in people's minds so they make bad choices which will separate them from the One who created them. God doesn't want to lose any...think about how one would feel to lose a child. All of those who have forsaken Him must be heartrending to our Savior. He never gives up on us, though, and is very patient with His children when they rebel or when they are slow to get the message

Today, through GLC (God's Learning Channel) He is repeating His Word over and over in a way (GLC programmers) which catches the attention of people like you and me, who have most likely been convicted by Him to watch the program. You see why I say every day, "Thank you, Jesus for choosing me!" And, you are probably reading this book because you are going through the same steps He is taking me through-where my obsession is for more... more of HIS WORD, and more of HIM...which are one and the same. Now, when I read my Bible, the verses seem to reinforce what I hear in Sunday school, at Worship Service, at Bible Study, on GLC...even in the songs we sing in ESL (English as a Second Language).

Most of the messages from all of these places seem to be pointing to a bringing together of Jew and Gentile into a new man of Christ...a restoration, if you will, of man as the image of God...His people of one mind, one soul, and one belief...ready for THE NEW JERUSALEM... where there will be no sin, no trials or tribulation... CAN YOU BELIEVE IT? NO EVIL!

I've always known we're supposed to be ready for His coming, and thought I was... however, He has opened my mind and heart through this writing that we need to read more scripture, pray unceasingly, listen for God's will, and "tell" anyone God sends into our vicinity...talk about Him to your relatives, your friends, your enemies, to strangers, to bosses, to colleagues; in other words, everyone.

John 4:35 "I tell you, open your eyes and look at the fields! They are ripe for harvest."

If you do this..."tell" everyone you meet about Jesus...you are in the clear. If those you have told about Jesus decide not to accept God's Grace, you are not at fault.

But, if you don't obey His command, and don't tell someone whom He sends to you, and they remain ignorant as to what is at stake...eternal life...because you neglected to tell them, then you will be held accountable.

So, don't be afraid to do your duty...you might be surprised at the reaction...the worst that could happen to you is that the person might turn his back and walk away. The best that could happen is that the person is ready to listen and accept Jesus. When someone says, "Yes, I would like to accept Jesus as my personal Savior," you will feel such joy that it is difficult to come off "cloud 9" long enough to finish your witness and assure him that to become "born again"...a new person in the Lord... he needs to confess his sins (not to you, but to Christ Jesus), be sorry for those sins, then, ask Him to come into his heart. AND HE DOES! He does not have to wait 'til he "cleans up his act." The Holy Spirit does that for him through "sanctification"... a process that is ongoing until we are IN THE NEW JERUSALEM. Then, we will all know the "rest of the story." WHAT A PROMISE! Nothing in this world can match it.

Perhaps a person has been cynical and wants to be shown proof of all of these promises of God; therein lays the "catch." This is where you tell him he must have FAITH that all of these promises ARE in the Bible and they will become real to him without proof if he reads and studies scriptures (it helps to pray first asking to understand them.)

GOD IS SO GOOD! Every time you come into His presence, He "grows" (sanctifies) you and provides just the "proof" you need for that day (a "quiet time" in your closet or in a hidden place where there are no distractions, where you can forget the worldly obligations or trials of the day is the best way to welcome His presence).

This is why it took me so long to have an actual "personal relationship" with Him; I was too busy, busy, busy. AND selfish, selfish, selfish. I didn't want to give up my "self-indulgent" behavior because I fell for the worldly advertising about "pleasing self being the goal of my existence."

One eventually sees that that goal is hollow (empty) and does not satisfy those inexplicable longings somewhere inside that never seemed to be fulfilled. One's life becomes tangled and chaotic until something catastrophic happens...like a divorce or a terminal illness or the death of a child...and one doesn't have anywhere to turn for answers. That's when we begin to be serious about going to church, reading our Bible, and/or praying...maybe not in that order...but we are beginning to see something is missing in our life.

We are beginning to determine only Jesus can give us the kind of love that fills the missing part in our being. Only JESUS CAN SATISFY those longings...which brings me to a cherished hymn of mine:

³SATISFIED WITH JESUS

(1) I am satisfied with Jesus; He has done so much for me;

He has suffered to redeem me; He has died to set me free.

CHORUS: I am satisfied, I am satisfied, I am satisfied with Jesus.

But the question comes to me, as I think of Calvary
Is my Master satisfied with me?

(2) He is with me in my trials; Best of friends of all is He;
I can always count on Jesus--Can He always count on me? (CHORUS)

(3) I can hear the voice of Jesus, calling out so pleadingly,

"Go and win the lost and straying"; Is He satisfied with me? (CHORUS)

(4) When my work on earth is ended, and I cross the mystic sea,

Oh, that I could hear Him saying, "I am satisfied with thee." (CHORUS)³

"Satisfaction" and "happiness" are two words hard to define...at least by the world's standards. But, if you have made Jesus THE LORD OF YOUR LIFE, He gives you both...no problem defining the words then...Jesus IS your satisfaction AND your happiness. Everything else in your life falls into place! Sure, you might have chaos (trials) now and then...no problem...He is with you through whatever. What a comforting thought...keep thinking thoughts like these while you are telling everyone you meet every day how He loves you and has provided you not only withcontentment and joy, but PEACE.

Isaiah 26:3 You will keep him in perfect

peace, whose mind is stayed on You, because he trusts in You.

John 14:27 Peace I leave with you; my peace I give to you. Not as the world gives do I give to you. Let not your hearts be troubled, neither let them be afraid.

John 16:33 "These things I have spoken to you, that in Me you may have peace. In the world you will have tribulation; but be of good cheer, I have overcome the world."

Romans 5:1 "Therefore, since we have been justified by faith, we have peace with God through our Lord Jesus Christ.

Psalm 35:9 Then my soul will rejoice in the Lord and delight in His salvation.

Read on... See how Jesus will give you the peace and joy He has given me.

PREPARING FOR THE NEW JERUSALEM

The first time I was aware of a "new" Jerusalem was probably not even a year ago...it's as if Jesus woke me up from my slumbering state at 75 years of age.

Because Revelation is a book of the Bible that is very difficult to understand, and because I left it until the very last, many times it was bypassed to read other more interesting chapters while attempting to read through the Bible in one year. This time, though, remembering how many of the verses brought to my attention lately had been mostly prophecy, I vowed to read through Revelation after praying for the Lord to make it clear to me.

This verse jumped out at me—**Revelation 3:12 Him who overcomes I will make a pillar in the temple of my God. Never again will he leave it. I will write on him the name of my God and the name of the city of my God, the New Jerusalem. Which is coming down out of heaven from my God; and I will also write on him My new name.**

Then, I continued, and read...**verse 13 He who has an ear, let him hear what the Spirit says to the churches.**

My ear had never really heard what the Spirit was saying; and, I had never really understood until recently that each one of us is "the church"...we are the temple where the Spirit resides. Also, "him who overcomes" is talking about us when we overcome evil (put Satan behind us in the name of Jesus).

Thank you, Jesus, for removing the scales from my eyes and opening my ears to actually understand that every chapter, every verse in the Bible is related to Jesus and our relationship with Him. I'm hoping you, the reader, will come closer to Jesus and put your relationship with Him as your top priority.

My story might ring a bell with you; and perhaps you will see the urgency of "waking up" to the need for spending more time telling others about His Kingdom, and more time on our knees praying for our leaders, this country, and for Jerusalem, the city of our Judeo-Christian heritage.

As mentioned before, in hindsight, He has been preparing me for the New Jerusalem since before conception...

Growing up in the small town of Silvis, Illinois, was the usual story of, economically speaking, a middle-class girl-child, anxious to please, impulsive, but sincere in wanting to do right; and, sometimes mischievous, but never malicious, honest to a fault, but also curious to see how far one could tease without crossing an invisible line into fed-up irritability in the case of one's favorite people; namely, parents, teachers, two older brothers, and best friends.

The first thing I remember about my early childhood was running around the corner of our house on 16th street, barefooted, under dripping eaves, carefree in the pouring rain; then feeling a searing pain in my foot close to the underside of my big toe. When I looked down after a loud howl, the running streams of water from around my foot were red, unsurprising to my five-year-old mind, but devastating to my mother, who came running at the sound of my loud wail. After our rush to the Doctor, much agony over the six-or-so stitches, and a rebuke from him for running barefoot in the rain, he assured my Mother the glass was "mostly" all out and that my toe would survive.

(To this day, if I stub my toe and happen to even brush the scar from where my toe was stitched back on, it causes an excruciating pain for probably 30 seconds—perhaps a nudge from The Holy Spirit?) Did I learn any lessons from my experience? maybe to pick up broken glass whenever I saw it or not to take soda bottles (no cans at that time, only bottles) on the sidewalks where they might get broken.

The strange thing is...where did the glass come from? I don't remember having sodas at that young age or anytime soon after that, as money was tight and no one ever thought of charging anything except at the grocery store, where the weekly or monthly bill, depending upon "payday," was paid. Kids were never allowed to put anything on their parents' food bill. Credit cards were non-existent at that time, at least in my small-town, working-class neighborhood...and your handshake was still a bond for any kind of transaction. The people in our town (pop. About 3,000) did not tolerate "shysters" and word was passed about who was and who wasn't best to enlist for one's hard-earned dollars.

My parents never prayed--at least within my hearing. My understanding of God was that He was to be feared...which to my childish mind meant to be afraid of...if we didn't be good, He might send a lightning bolt down to strike us, and in my imaginative, unschooled (at least spiritually) thinking, that meant pain and embarrassment.

Every Sunday my Mom would wake us up early, fix a big breakfast, (usually pancakes and sausage), check behind our ears to be sure they were washed in our Saturday night bath (in the Midwest, showers hadn't caught on yet, mostly baths--at least in my area—so a thorough scrub with a "washrag" was our daily cleansing), then my two brothers and I would walk to Sunday School. My brother, Jerry, the younger of the two was to be responsible for me, his little bratty sister, who always followed him around, unless he was able to elude me somehow. (He was actually very kind to me most of the time, unless I tattled on him and Arnold to get in good with Mom...then, I was a "brat.")

As we all got older, my brother, Arnold, somehow persuaded Mom to let him sleep in. I would go to Sunday school with my best friend, Lois, to her church; my brother, Jerry, was faithful to attend Sunday school and all the youth activities where we had gone from the beginning. Being the only one who consistently heard an invitation to accept Jesus as his Personal Savior, Jerry became saved before either Arnold or me, even though he fell away from his conviction for a time during his trials (Which I will tell you more of later.)

Being woefully shy, my first awareness of even speaking up to answer the teacher's question in an oral discussion was in the eighth grade when my favorite teacher (even though everyone was afraid of her) gave smiles for correct answers and actually threw a book at a silly adolescent boy who never listened...therefore, never knew the answer to any question. The book missed its target, but, needless to state, everyone was awake and listening after that...even the good students improved their agility by ducking at the right time.

When I look back on those days, I now realize those big boys didn't really know English, so would be covering it up by trying to be wise guys to impress the girls. (Maybe that's why my mission today is to teach English to anyone interested every Thursday evening).

Miss Strom appointed me to help Manuel (the boy at whom she had flung the book) with lessons, although he had been the "bane" (problem) of my 13 yr.-old existence that year. (He teased all the girls.)

She bestowed confidence ON me, however, by showing confidence IN me; and, in our general assembly once a week, where we said the Pledge of Allegiance, sang the Star Spangled Banner, and listened to our Principal extol (praise) Patriotism and Godliness, I began to think God and country were supremely important and a necessary part of life if we were to be "successful."

One mistake I made at that young age,was to let God fade into the background of my activities and put myself and my desires in the foreground, and to crave glory for myaccomplishments, never realizing that any talents I have or accomplishments perceived were/are from HIM... and they were/are to be used for HIS glory.

In those days, the Golden Rule (to treat others like we wanted to be treated) was quite often the subject of our morning activities and of bulletin boards in our classroom. In high school, this became my mantra (oft repeated expression), and other students began to want to be my friend because I helped them to find their talents and complimented them until they gained some confidence (kind of like Miss Strom did for me).

My motives were suspect...as in the back of my mind, I loved the feeling of being sought out and recognized as a good friend and a "do-gooder." That recognition was my goal, and seemed to be uppermost in my mind instead of a selfless trust in God.

Do you ever really think about what the words say when you sing the old hymn, "Trust and Obey?"

Only recently they became more precious to me after the "Light bulb" clicked on...

[4]TRUST AND OBEY

(1) When we walk with the Lord in the LIGHT of HIS WORD
What a GLORY HE sheds on our way!
Let us do HIS good will; HE abides with us still,
And with all who will trust and obey.

CHORUS: Trust and obey, for there's no other way
To be happy in Jesus, but to trust and obey.

(2) Not a burden we bear, not a sorrow we share,
But our toil HE doth richly repay;
Not a grief or a loss, not a frown or a cross,
But is blest if we trust and obey. (Chorus)
(3) But we never can prove the delights of HIS love
Until all on the altar we lay;
For the favor HE shows and the joy HE bestows
Are for them who will trust and obey. (Chorus)
(4) Then in fellowship sweet, we will sit at His feet

Or we'll walk by His side in the way;
What HE says we will do, Where He sends we will go;
Never fear only trust and obey. (Chorus)

If you have never had the opportunity to sing it, just think about the story it tells.

In high school, there were students who resented my meddling with their followers...and we seemed to be in competition for the "friends' loyalty"...they would call me "Goody two shoes" and deride me every chance they could. In hindsight...most of my "enemies" were the ones who had cars, did "exciting" (in some of the kids' minds) things like drinking, smoking, drag-racing, and other daring activities late at night...probably received mediocre grades or failing grades, and seemed not to care. My praise now is for God; however, because He was with me even then, and I didn't know it. Several of those students were killed in car wrecks, had to get married because of pregnancies, and/or committed suicide before they came to the knowledge that they needed OUR SAVIOR in their lives.

Ironically, some of those "fast" kids went to the same University I did and became Sorority sisters of mine. We chalked up our high school rivalry to "kid stuff" and became good friends. I'm sorry to say, however, that without a conscious, continuing relationship with Jesus, my "Goody-two shoes" resistance to the temptations of college life fell by the wayside while I succumbed to the lure of "Big Band Music,""Cocktail Hour," and parties. (I sang with a group...a trumpet, Bass Fiddle, piano and

7

drums...didn't play in night clubs, though; only for the Greek Sororities/Fraternities' dances). Managing to make grades high enough to keep my scholarship, and finally realizing the "fast" lane was not where I wanted to be,(the Holy Spirit was convicting me to "give it up")—my second year, (when my Mom died) I began to get serious about getting an education.

"If you love me, you will obey what I command. And I will ask the Father, and He will give you another counselor to be with you forever--the Spirit of Truth... the world cannot accept Him because it neither sees Him nor knows Him. But you know Him, for He lives with you and will be in you." John 15:15-17 (PRAISE GOD!)

ARNOLD

My brother, Arnold, eight years older than I, played on the tennis team in high school (We had moved from 16th street to 11th street, on the top of the hill, across from the tennis courts and across a gully to the Silvis Park.) He practiced constantly with his friends and allowed me to shag the balls...even some which went over the fence way down into the dense undergrowth in the gully. When he had no one with whom to practice, he taught me the basics of tennis...how to hold the racket, (which at the time, was much too big in the grip for my small hand so I had to "choke up" on the racket) how to swing forehand, then backhand and finally how to serve.

(For my 10th birthday, after much coaxing, Mom bought me an inexpensive light-weight racket and after practicing with my friends and/or Arnold every year until I was a junior in high school, I made the girls' tennis team... thanks to my brother's lessons started at about eight years of age. I never thanked him enough for his help. Playing tennis was one of the pleasures God afforded me throughout much of my life.)

Arnold was a senior in high school when he went for a ride on the back of his friend, Lyle's motorcycle. It was late evening and they had no headlight. Arnold was using a flashlight whenever they saw a car coming. He had turned off the flashlight to conserve the battery when from nowhere a car appeared with no headlights. Lyle tried to swerve away from the sideswipe, but snagged the passenger (with one grip of the handlebar) laying on the fender of the car using a flashlight in the same manner. The boy, a friend of theirs, was flipped off the fender and somersaulted onto the road, but, praise-the-Lord, not run over by either of the vehicles. He had many cuts and bruises and a bad concussion, from which he eventually recovered. Arnold had a broken wrist and ankle...his friend, Lyle, was broken up in several places. After wearing two casts for three months, Arnold grudgingly admitted Mom was right about not letting him have a motorcycle six months before when he was so angry at Mom and Dad for not being able to afford a motorcycle (mostly because they didn't want him to kill himself.) I believe God sent Angels to protect those boys.

Arnold went off to war (enlisted in the navy as soon as he was graduated from high school), and even though WW2 was winding down, and the Armistice was to be signed, he was on a ship that was in the Pacific theater, which meant they were finding "enemy" troops on the islands who didn't realize the war was over and were still defending their positions. Evidently, that was their mission...to get the word to every remote island where radios might have been destroyed or, for some reason, the troops in hiding, friendly or hostile, had not been notified. He was one of the weathermen on the ship and used balloons and other instruments to keep the ships and islands in the area informed about weather conditions in that part of the Pacific.

So, when Arnold came home after two-and-one-half years on the high seas, his main thought was to "make up for lost time". He proceeded to sow some very wild oats, deciding to marry several years later when his first child was expected. This didn't interfere with his sowing;

however, I believe his wife's (and others') prayers finally convinced God to intervene, and Arnold began to clean up his act, show his wife he truly loved her, and sow more spiritual "oats"...ironically, a "denomination" contrary to his wife's beliefs. She accepted this answer to prayer, however, giving thanks that Arnold had turned from his various iniquities to a fervent work for God's Kingdom.

Devote yourselves to prayer, being watchful and thankful. Colossians 4:2

Their arguments were no longer about his late nights out, but were now mostly about Jesus and His role in their lives. They read the same Bible, but could not always come to the same conclusions about much of anything... except the most important bottom line--that Jehovah is our Creator and that He loves His people and wants all to love Him and their neighbors as themselves. So, they agreed in mutual understanding that God,love, and respect were the ingredients most needed in their marriage and in any marriage.

His wife, Bonnie, was to be one of my mentors who set me back on the narrow path to Jesus. When she passed away in 1997, many of her "chicks" realized what a powerful influence she had been in their lives for Jesus, and only wished they had let her know how much she was loved.Arnold has these same regrets; however, Bonnie's strength in the Lord and her constant example of faith in Jesus has turned his regrets into joy when he finally acknowledged Jesus as his Lord and Savior and began to have a personal relationship with Jesus. I believe that lady has many crowns and is rejoicing with Jesus every time one of her "chicks" is back on track.

Bonnie often talked about God's promises:

Good Health

He who dwells in the shelter of the Most High will rest in the shadow of the Almighty. I will say of the Lord, "He is my refuge and my fortress, my God in whom I trust." Surely He will save you from the fowler's (Satan) snare (trap) and from the deadly pestilence (disease and bad health). (my parenthesis**)Psalms 91:1-3**

When I was struck with a deadly disease (in those days, no antibiotics to speak of) called "Scarlet Fever,"at the age of about seven, my parents thought I was going to die. My throat seemed to be closing up; I couldn't catch my breath. The family Doctor (only one for the whole town of Silvis) came immediately and gave me shots directly into my stomach...that's the only thing I remember about that illness--those scary shots into my stomach! He came every day for five days and administered more shots.

I can't recall anyone praying over me or telling me to pray--so I assumed no one did. However, I recovered--so, maybe my Mom and Dad prayed in the quiet of their room...or maybe they asked someone to pray for me--or maybe Jesus prayed to the Father for me--He was there with me...because most kids who contracted that disease in those days did not survive; and I know nowHe had a purpose for my life.

With this in mind, we constantly pray for you, that our God may count you worthy of His calling, and that by His power he may fulfill every good purpose of yours and

every act prompted by your faith. We pray this so that the name of our Lord Jesus may be glorified in you, and you in Him, according to the grace of our God and the Lord Jesus Christ. 2nd Thes 1:11,12

Since that time, I have been healthy...it just wasn't a practice of our family to run to a doctor for every little sniffle. If any in our family suggested sluggishness, my Mother had two remedies...first, a laxative (milk-of-magnesia--ugh!), second, Cod-liver oil (one teaspoon every day). If there were signs of a cold (flu wasn't even mentioned in those days except on a very rare occasion), she immediately rubbed Vicks Vapor Rub on the chest and made us put Vicks as far up in our nostrils as possible. Then, we stayed in bed until we were back to normal (in her eyes). This regimen discouraged us from even thinking about faking illness to get out of something we considered unpleasant (like work around the house or a test at school for which we hadn't studied) because Mom's very effective treatment was worse than the alternative...so we learned from an early age to face each hardship (in our eyes) and to be sure to do any homework necessary to get good grades.

Thurman Scrivner (on GLC) is giving us scriptures that have God's promises concerning DIVINE HEALTH. With much faith and prayer and walking with Jesus, we can claim those promises and have good health without prescribed medicines which tend to cause more bad health from man-made medicine's continual assault on other organs.

Several years ago. I bought a little book called, THE PROMISES OF GOD, glanced through it when I first bought it; and then was distracted, so set it aside for later.

However, before I could really study it, God sent someone to me who needed it more than I did... plus, I could always pick up another one at a Bible book shop. Four years later, when I was given another copy of the same little book, read it, andrealized all those years God's promises could have been mine. Claim those promises now, before it is too late!

God is good and He keeps His promises! But you do have to stay in His will and ASK Him for good health, and be sure to ask HIS FORGIVENESS for any sins you have committed that day—like getting angry and yelling at someone, or telling a small "fib" to your spouse or children; remember, a sin is a sin—none are any worse than the other in Jesus's eyes.

Thurman Srivner emphasizes that "unforgiven sin" from years past or yesterday can cause illness, both physically and spiritually. Your evening prayer can incorporate your repentance for your "failure" in pleasing Jesus. Yes, He died for our sins; we've already been forgiven...but, that acknowledgement each day to Jesus that we know we did wrong and that He will forgive us is what keeps us mentally and spiritually healthy, and subsequently physically healthy. I believe it; mostly because of my own experience...with my feet. More about that later.

Believers, But...

My Mother always cooked us a good breakfast, mostly soup and/or sandwiches for lunch, and meat and potatoes for "supper" (as it was called in the Midwest); and when it was ready, we were called to come to the table. We ate together as a family. I don't remember saying a prayer before each meal; however, I do believe both of my parents were believers who had simply forgotten the needto acknowledge God as their Savior and Provider. (A good friend of mine mentioned to me about 30 years ago that if you pray before every meal or anytime you eat--even a snack—asking God for nourishment--the food will never make you sick—what he said is true, according to my experience.)

When I look back on our young lives...one of the reasons I was not aware of the necessity for reading and understanding God's Word and living by His Word was...my parents seemed unable or too self-conscious to demonstrate any deep feeling to each other and to us, though we always knew they loved us. The only thing I ever saw them reading was a secular magazine, LADIES' HOME JOURNAL, or a newspaper now and then. I didn't even realize we had a Bible until my Mother passed away on Thanksgiving morning when I was nineteen years old. My Father had put the large white "family" Bible on the coffee table in the living room the day before I came home from college for Thanksgiving vacation.

(I had no idea my Mom was that ill; and, the past September, when school commenced, had been told to

go back to Macomb, about 75 miles away, for my second year of college.)

When my Mom died, my world seemed to have dropped out from under me, as I had no clue that I could have turned to my heavenly Father at that time when feeling so empty and "lost." No one in my household, including visiting aunts and uncles at the funeral, ever mentioned God, prayer, or heaven...or if they did, I spaced it out... because my guilt for not staying home from college that year and being with my Mom her last few months didn't leave me for many years...until I finally learned that I could turn it over to Jesus (that was almost twenty years later). If only I had known Jesus more intimately then...

Though He brings grief, He will show compassion, so great is His unfailing love. Lamentations 3:32

There was something about people in the Midwest back in those days (and probably still today) that God was only mentioned in church when and if one went every Sunday morning. No one showed deep passion for Christ...actually, it seemed to be bad manners to show any deep emotion about anything because it would embarrass someone in your vicinity. Praise God, when I finally moved out west, there were people who appreciated hugs and fervent feelings for our Creator; 'cause I soon found my earliest Sunday School lessons coming back to the forefront of my mind and was finally able to turn my life over to Jesus (after I had four children and had been divorced from my first husband, whom I had made my God for 20 years).

Train a child in the way he should go, and when he is old, he will not turn from it. Proverbs 22:6

JERRY

My brother, Jerry, who was the most compassionate one of the whole family, was very sensitive and was hurt more often than he would admit. God was very real to him, and Jerry had very tender skin about his relationship with Jesus. I often mistook his bravado for not caring; however, he was the one who always came through for whoever was needy in the family--physically or emotionally. He worked at the movie theater from the age of 14...from popcorn popper to usher to manager before he was a senior in high school, and usually spent his earnings on presents for everyone's birthday or Christmas.

Jerry didn't lose his adolescent chubbiness until he was about 16 years old--when he had a growth spurt. All of a sudden, he began to notice girls...or maybe they began to notice him. After graduating from high school, he decided to marry his high school sweetheart (who was still in high school), and they moved in to a basement apartment in our folks' home.

Mother-in-law troubles began when Jerry's teen-age wife didn't live up to my Mom's expectations. (I learned at that time more than one family should not live in the same household). Jerry decided to join the Marines, went to California for Boot training; and later, when he became an expert shot, was promoted and assigned to train recruits. He wasn't sent overseas with his outfit, so was able to obtain housing on the base for him and his wife, whom he moved out there on his first furlough.

He admitted to me later that neither he nor his first wife were mature enough to take on the responsibility of marriage and children, nor did they have the spiritual knowledge that God needed to be first in their lives rather than indulging in satisfying "self" at the risk of the demise (death) of their marriage. It was even before the divorce that Jerry began to sow his wild oats and pushed God further into the background of his life.

When he married Alice, he seemed to reform somewhat; however,as did his earthly father, Jerry began to spend evenings in different taverns, supposedly selling insurance to bar owners and night club owners, drinking sometimes into the wee hours of the morning. When our Dad sold his insurance business (which he had built up with Jerry's help), he bought a small night club from one of his insurance clients who was ready to retire, and gave it to Jerry to run.(Dad was still working eight hours a day for the Rock Island Railroad).

After several years of tolerating his late closing time and the smell of liquor permeating his clothing if not his whole being, Alice gave Jerry an ultimatum...get out of this business or lose her. He described to me later that his life behind a bar serving drinks to "drunks", what he had become himself, was a "quicksand pit" into which he was slowly being dragged down to "Hell on earth", and knew it was only a matter of time before he was "lost and gone forever."

They bought several acres in Missouri—about 200 miles from the unhappy times—and Jerry proceeded to build them a house. Carpentry was his first love and I believe Jesus used it to bring Jerry back to the fold. Their marriage survived, but only when they returned back to the earth and had to depend on the Lord for sustenance. With a few cows and a prolific garden (Alice had a very green thumb), they prayed together and worked hard on the land, until Jerry finally turned from the liquor back to Jesus, Who had never left Jerry...it was Jerry who had strayed from Jesus.

To supplement their income, Jerry used the ability God had given him building cabinets for the businesses that were springing up around their area.When I look back, it was evident that Jerry was much blessed by the Lord... being very bright, honest, and sincere--a high achiever in whatever he undertook. I would say Jerry was like Joseph; and like Joseph, never realized his worth until later when he grew even closer to the Lord. Praise God, Mark, our son, in his adolescent teen- age years, at a breaking point from "Mr. Hyde's" demonic behavior and the constant stress in the family, jumped on a bus to Missouri to stay with Jerry and Alice for several weeks on the farm. Jerry exemplified to Mark how an earthly Father was supposed to be. Our Father, God, had sent an angel to Mark to keep him from stubbing his toe.

Psalm91:9-12If you make the Most High your dwelling—even the Lord, Who is my refuge—then no harm will befall you, no disaster will come near your tent. For He will command the angels concerning you to guard you in all your ways, they will lift you up in their hands, so that you will not strike your foot against a stone.

Not realizing at the time how much Mark was bearing the brunt of his Dad's manic-depressive illness, (when I was escaping with Katrina) plus how much peer pressure was on Mark from some of the other teen-age boys who found an "escape" from their own family problems in alcohol and drugs, I was mostly concerned that he was missing school. Praise God for His watch-care.

Jerry and Alice folded him in their arms and treated Mark as if he were the son they never had. Jerry displayed his love for fine carpentry to Mark and, I realize now, his love of the Master Carpenter through his example. If only I had truly emptied "self" and been filled with the Holy Spirit then, I might have known the angels had spirited Mark to Jerry for safekeeping.

Thank you, Lord, for giving me a brother who was truly yours.He was "ready" last year when the Lord called him home.

By telling you short biographies of my brothers, you may see how their influence shaped my opinions for many years because we were all three raised by the same God-fearing parents, although we lost our beloved Mom at age 47 to cancer--which means we didn't wake up soon enough to tell her how much we loved and appreciated her care. Open affection was never evident in our house, most likely because none of us took the time to converse with each other, or really got to know each other...never prayed together or read the Bible together... too much concerned with things of the "world" and too busy pleasing self until quite late in our lives when we finally came to the conclusion that we needed Jesus to straighten out our thinking. Hope you came to that conclusion before we did.

(One other Mentor the Lord supplied to Mark during those crucial years was Mel Root, my Superintendent at Maxwell School at the time. When Mr. Hyde took off to

Mexico one summer with our credit card, Mel and Jan, his wife, invited me to help out at their summer camp as a counselor to theyoungestgroup of girl campers. That was the first of 13 summers when all four of my children enjoyed camp activities such as horseback trail rides, hiking--at first short hikes then, the final grand hike to the top of Hermit's peak--Sunday services sitting cross-legged under a tree, as well as ending each day around the campfire with songs and prayer before going off to our cabins. As Mark grew into his latter teens, Mel gave him more responsibility around the camp--giving him the confidence to be able to help maintain the plumbing, re-bark the outside of the cabins, shingle the leaking roofs—as well as being a counselor to the younger boys and, later, to the teen-aged boys. Mel and Jan, an awakened Christian couple, shaped much of Mark's love of the Master Carpenter; and those wholesome summers in the mountains gave a glimpse of life with Jesus to all of us.)

No Coincidences with God

My awareness of God actually sending angels to protect His family didn't dawn on me until recently, within the past ten years. Things that happened that seemed supernatural could always be explained away as being "co-incidence." Being "too busy studying" or "working on lesson plans" or "grading papers" to read the Bible (which I didn't take off to college with me 'cause I didn't even own one), later was an answer to my conscience (which was the Holy Spirit nudging me).

When five of my Sorority sisters and I were traveling to an out-of-town football game, and a car came into our lane straight at us, and was not getting back into his lane, all six of us were praying mightily that God would direct JoAnn's hands on the steering wheel, as it took quick thinking and reacting to know which way the driver would correct himself...if she had chosen to veer right, we would have had a head-on collision and probably all been killed, because in those days, there were seatbelts in very few cars.

But, she pulled left and straight across onto the shoulder of the oncoming lane...in which there was no car coming... praise the Lord! The other car ran into the ditch on our side of the road. After it was over and we called the police from a nearby farmhouse (no cell phones yet), we were informed that the man was drunk and had been driving erratically for some time before he passed out at the wheel. We all agreed on how lucky we had been; but, forgot to credit God for answering our "emergency" prayer.

These kinds of happenings were sporadic throughout my life; and, now I can see where He was with me in every situation...and, now I know He (the Holy Spirit) has been there all the time--which reminds me of another of my favorite hymns,

5HE WAS THERE ALL THE TIME.

Read the words to this song by Gary S. Paxton...
(1). Time after time I went searching for peace in some void,
I was trying to blame all my ills on this world I was in
Surface relationships used me till I was done in,
And all the while someone was begging to free me from sin.

CHORUS: He was there all the time, He was there all the time...
Waiting patiently in line, He was there all the time.
(2). Never again will I look for a fake rainbow's end,
Now that I have the answer, my life is just startingto rhyme;
Sharing each new day with him is a cup of new life,
O what I missed! He's been waiting right there all the time.
These words are my story in a "nutshell"...possibly yours, also, and even though unsaved or saved, in your heart you know them to be true because you're reading this book. If you've never asked Jesus into your heart, DO IT NOW! HE'S THERE...WAITING.

Mindset of Jesus

If you ARE saved, and He IS your personal intimate Friend, and you converse with Him every day, then you might say, "I've been forgiven for all my mistakes when I found Jesus--I don't need to be reminded of my past." But, with all the distractions of an evil world, we sometimes need to be reminded to have the"mindset of Jesus." I know I do, especially the part of sharing each new day with Him so we can have"cup of new life" (filled with the Holy Spirit) to fortify us for daily living in a hostile world.

He is preparing us for the New Jerusalem by changing our thinking...(our "mindset", if you will). When we truly think like Him, for Him, and with Him, then we are becoming ready for the New Jerusalem.

Acts 4:32 All the believers were one in heart and mind.

When our thinking is:
1)*immersed in Him; relying on Him; The Holy Spirit controlling all thoughts.*
2) Oftentimes about our Jewish Roots.
3) Attuned to others (with God's mindset) in God's Kingdom.
4) Never worldly thinking (block the "Deceiver" out, in Jesus' name).
5) OBEDIENCE to God being uppermost in our thinking.

At one time, before I actually read the Bible, my thoughts were influenced by whatever comments were in the news at that time; oftentimes those comments were anti-Christian and sometimes indicated that whatever you wanted to do was all right as long as you didn't hurt someone else...called "situational ethics." Even today, many so-called scholars promote the premise that the Old Testament is no longer relevant because it was written for "those" times rather than for "today." Some pseudo-intellectuals like to pontificate their theories about the "real" motives behind different Truths in the Bible, confusing those who have no knowledge of the Bible other than what they hear from preachers, News commentators, and celebrities. These "scholars" read many books, do much studying, and much thinking-- consequently, they feel this qualifies them to question the inerrant Word of God. These "False Teachers", who take away from or add to the Bible are cursed by the Holy God and need to repent before it is too late.

Ecclesiastes 12:12-13 Be warned, my son, of anything in addition to them (the words of the Bible).Of making many books there is no end, and much study wearies the body. Let us hear the conclusion of the whole matter: Fear God, and keep His commandments, for this is the whole duty of man. (my parenthesis)

Think about it! The word "fear" can mean other things than "being afraid of." It can mean "respect." Both fear and respect promote obedience—which is what God expects from us so He can give us all the promised blessings talked about in the Bible.

Fearing God is the duty of man...He created us. He made the family setup for our good...so the earthly father could pattern his behavior after the Heavenly Father; and provide his wife and children with the love and caring our Heavenly Father showers on us daily.

Ephesians 5:25 Husbands, love your wives, even as Christ also loved the church, and gave himself for it. *(The "church" is the true believerswho have Jesus in their hearts.)*

Any caring father will discipline his errant children as our Heavenly Father disciplines us...thereby the fear—because we respect our fathers enough that we fear their displeasure. Our earthly fathers need to discipline in love, however, and set good examples for their children so they earn the respect it takes for them to firmly discipline a child who needs guidance. If the child fears his/her father because he is cruel and unloving, that kind of fear does not render respect...only resentment...and oftentimes rebellion, which only leads to violence, not love.

If an earthly father knows Jesus and has a personal relationship with Him, he will be the example his family needs to nurture loving, caring family relationships; however, the "Deceiver" has many worldly weapons to use against people who are trying to be "in this world, but not of this world."

Thankfully, Jesus has promised us discernment...the ability to recognize true words from Jesus (not to fall for the promises of the "Father of Lies") and the ability to know other true members of the Family of God...IF we continuepraying, reading, and following the Bible (God's instruction Book), which is the main weapon of the Christian. This is the message we must emphasize in these latter days.

Also, you understand and gain knowledge of the Word by hearing. That's why we have Sunday School and Worship Service on Sunday morning and Bible Study on

Sunday and Wednesday evenings. He has promised that whenever two or more come together in My Name, He will be there also.

Matthew 18:20 "For where two or three are gathered together in My name, I am there in the midst of them."

The Family of God

And when He knocks on the door of your heart, and you invite Him into your heart and are sincerely repentant for past sins, you become a true member of the Family of God and want to tell everyone, thereby confessing Him before men.

"Therefore whoever confesses Me before men, him I will also confess before My Father Who is in heaven." Matthew 10:32

Having known this vaguely in the back of my mind from my kindergarten days, it was probably taught to me in my Baptist Sunday school lessons; but having run the gamut of Baptist (about ages 4 to 9), Methodist (about ages 10 to 19), Roman Catholic (about ages 20 to 42), back to roots and an actual relationship with Jesus Christ, my true salvation came at a late stage of my life...I didn't answer the invitation to "walk the aisle" until age 44. The very sad reality of all those early years, moving from one church to another...not once was there an open invitation to accept Jesus as Lord, at least while I was attending the Sunday services—perhaps my ears were not "hearing" at that time.

Praise the Lord for sending Jack (my second husband) to

guide me back to the Bible and a Bible- preaching church, and Pastors who issue an invitation at every worship service. Praise the Lord for John and Christie Van Sweden, who I'm sure prayed me into a closer relationship with Jesus, and provided the setting of their ranch, riding horses, and gathering cattle to draw me closer to Jack.

Even though I was a "baby" Christian for several years after that, my Lord, Jesus Christ was with me; and I was like a kid in love for the first time. That kind of enthusiasm is what Jesus honors, and He has brought me a long way in a short time (at least the way Hekeeps time). *We are still being "purified" (sanctified, refined, honed, set-apart) and will continue to be until The New Jerusalem.*

I am Not Ashamed (of the Gospel): Lately, the message from several different sources has been, *"I am not ashamed." The ad on TV goes on to say..."I am not ashamed of the Gospel of Jesus Christ." Hallelujah! Christians are speaking out. They are confessing Him before men and the world! More and more are becoming unashamed and are "coming out of the closet" about their love for Jesus and for their brothers and sisters in Christ.

1st John 4:15 Whoever confesses that Jesus is the son of God, God abides in him, and he in God.

Romans 10:9) that if you confess with your mouth Jesus as Lord, and believe in your heart that God raised Him from the dead, you shall be saved; 10) For with the heart man believes, resulting in righteousness, and with the mouth he confesses, resulting in salvation.

Romans 1:16, 17 For I am not ashamed of the gospel of Christ, for it is the power of God to salvation for everyone who believes, for the Jew first and also for

the Greek. For in it the righteousness of God is revealed from faith to faith, as it is written, "The just shall live by faith."

God is putting a great hunger in many for Him--THE WORD, THE TRUTH, AND THE LIGHT.

Jesus said in the beatitudes, "Blessed are those who hunger and thirst for righteousness." He also said, "Blessed are the pure in heart, for they shall see God."Matthew 5:6,8

This, then should be our major goal; and, with the help of the Holy Spirit prayed into our being every day, it is possible to keep our hearts pure and hungering for more and more of JESUS.

Below is an old hymn written in 1932, two years before I was born...especially relevant today...I'LL TELL THE WORLD THAT I'M A CHRISTIAN. An old hymn with a message for "sleeping" Christians (like I was for so long):

[4]I'LL TELL THE WORLD THAT I'M A CHRISTIAN

1 I'll tell the world that I'm a Christian--I'm not ashamed
    His name to bear;
I'll tell the world that I'm a Christian--I'll take Him with
    me anywhere.
I'll tell the world how Jesus saved me, and how He gave
    me a life brand new;
And I know that if you trust Him, that all He gave me, He'll
    give to you.
I'll tell the world that He's my Saviour, no other one could
    love me so;
My life, my all is His forever, and where He leads me, I
    will go.

2 I'll tell the world that He is coming--it may be near or far away;
But we must live as if His coming would be tomorrow or today.
For when He comes and life is over, for those who love Him, there's more to be;
Eyes have never seen the wonders that He's preparing for you and me.
O tell the world that you're a Christian—be not ashamed His name to bear
O tell the world that You're a Christian—and take Him with you everywhere.

When He's in your life; in fact, when He is your first love, your guide, your Savior, your Lord...you will be anxious NOT to disappoint Him. And, you will want to tell everyone about receiving the Grace of God.

As John MacArthur quotes in his book, [6]THE GOSPEL ACCORDING TO JESUS, "Clearly, grace does not grant permission to live in the flesh (which would disappoint our Savior very, very much); it supplies power to live in the Spirit. Those who reject 'Lordship salvation' stumble over the twin truths that salvation is a gift, YET IT COSTS EVERYTHING." (My caps and parenthetical expression).

When he says, "It costs everything"...be not dismayed; because...**Romans 16:26 "He brings us to faith, then ENABLES and EMPOWERS us to believe unto obedience."** (What a promise!) We could never do it alone!

PRAISE GOD! HE IS SO GOOD!

Oh, but beloved, we all need to be reminded of His

blessings and that He is in control...mainly so we don't let the "Deceiver" think he can take the place of our "Abba,"(Father), especially when we're so busy we forget to give God the glory for everything...even in the trials we have. Remember, God uses those "trials" to keep SANCTIFYING, REFINING, and PREPARING US FOR THE NEW JERUSALEM.

I digress...back to my story:

Middletown

When I was teaching in Middletown, New York, my main goal in life was to "stand out" as an exemplary teacher and please all of the people all of the time. It did not enter my mind that that "secular" goal was impossible to achieve; nor did it enter my mind or heart to please Jesus, because I did not know him, even though I thought I was being a good Christian by going to Mass once in a while.

(I had switched to Roman Catholic when I thought I was going to marry Tony, my college sweetheart, who had become a West Point cadet my second year of college. After some correspondence the following several years, he invited me to his graduation ball at the Point...whereupon I applied for a teaching job and was hired in Middletown, close to the West Point Academy. It was a premature move, because subsequently, at the ball, we found that we no longer had anything in common and parted amiably. However, the girls' physical education position turned out to be "right up my alley," and I thrived on teaching soccer, hockey, dance, and trampoline to freshman and sophomore girls.)

On "College Night" at Middletown High School (60 miles north of NYC), all teachers were asked to host a recruiter from the different colleges from all over the U.S.I was assigned to host a recruiter from a Woman's College in Ohio.

(Each teacher prepared a room with projector, board, chalk, pencils and pens for filling out applications, etc.)

Expecting a young woman recruiter from a woman's college, I was totally surprised when a tall, dark- haired older man came into the room, walked right over to me, took my hands and introduced himself. (I forgot to say a very handsome, square-jawed man). After a few seconds of his deep blue eyes looking straight into my eyes, he finally let go of my hands. I was a bit flustered, and all I could think of was, "Thank goodness, the students aren't in the room yet!"

In those days, it was frowned upon for a teacher to show any signs of having a life outside of the classroom. (The premise was...teachers were to be teachers not peers, engendering more respect). But I did realize there was a spark between us at that first meeting.

Yes, your guess is correct...we were married the following June, of 1958...after a whirlwind courtship. We always laughed about "love at first sight;" but it did seem to be true in our case, even though the spark was eventually dampened after four children...and the realism of life set in when we finally settled in a place where we stayed longer than the usual two years.

Getting married to a man whom I hardly knew was exciting, but eye-opening to an inexperienced, basically shy, undemonstrative

23 yr.-old woman...also immature to the ways of the world and still in the "self" mode of life.

Looking back on those courtship days from this far in the future, we had been together only about a month's worth of days before we were married (when Gerald could get back to Middletown from wherever he was recruiting, or Whenever I could travel on Saturdays or Sundays to join him). The pleasure of being together was exhilarating, though, and we enjoyed each other's company...seemed to have so much to talk about, and he impressed me mightily with his super intelligence. However, we never discussed whether or not he believed in the Lord, or if he wanted children, or if he could support a family; or anything about the responsibilities of living.

He was 32 years old at the time; and, in my eyes, a handsome older man was much more fascinating and eligible than a young, callow, (inexperienced) West Point Cadet just graduated from the Military Academy. What I didn't understand was that by age 32, and never married, many men are already set in their ways--habits and activities, mentality and attitudes. It had escaped my notice that whenever we joined each other, Gerald always chose a restaurant or club where he could have drinks with the meal.

Because I had never developed a personal relationship with Jesus before that time, the fact that Gerald never mentioned God or Jesus or the Holy Spirit did not seem extraordinary to me. I was not in the habit of praying (only when I needed something) or even talking about "religion" then...so, it did not seem obvious that he never talked about his "faith". I guess I just assumed he believed in God. So, from October to June, we met now and then, and married, (to me, a fairy-tale wedding)on June 21st of 1958, in East Moline, Illinois, at St. Anne's Catholic Church. Everything about the Church service was perfect. The reception afterward, however, was a catastrophy.

Drinks were served with dinner at the Country Club; and as time went on, Gerald was showing a contempt for our "homespun" planning. I hadn't been aware of his need for perfection (his idea of perfection) until then; and I believe he drank more than he might have if he thought our plans were just as he wanted them. (Little did I know that one drink of gin could put him into that mode of thinking.)

Gerald and I drove my shiny new robin's-egg blue Chevy convertible coupe ('57—after one year of teaching without a car, my dad signed for me to purchase my first car the summer before so I could drive it out to New York)from Illinois to Mexico, Missouri, where we spent the first night of our honeymoon. Since we planned to drive all the way to Acapulco, Mexico, touring; staying in a small Missouri burg called "Mexico" the first night was a humorous "conversation piece" for when we returned. (He took pride in doing and saying unusual things to cause admiration for his uniqueness...almost to the point of being obsessive.) The champagne and gin he had consumed at the wedding reception, however, had caused his behavior to be much too bizarre for me in my bridal timidity, and I wondered if I had married "Mr. Hyde" rather than Dr. Jekyll--later finding out "Mr. Hyde" appeared whenever martinis (gin) were on the menu. (Jekyll & Hyde are equated with a "split personality" in literature.)

Having never seen that side of him during our few days of

courtship, I became regretfully aware of it on my wedding night. Being ready to go back home in the morning, obtain an annulment, and never see him again ever, his profusely apologetic, endearing hang-dog look (straight into my eyes--tender and loving) convinced me his promise to never, ever be that way again was genuine.

Professing to be a Christian, I decided to take him at his word, and vowed to "stick it out"...and, when "Dr. Jekyll" was present (which was most of the time, at first) we seemed the ideal couple, especially when we were teaching overseas, having a variety of new experiences to satisfy Gerald's obsessive need for the "unusual."

Wefound an apartment in Middletown; I taught Physical Education for one more year, while Gerald was traveling around the U.S. to various high schools recruiting girls for the Ohio Women's College. Being apart was difficult; but when we did have a weekend together, our time was precious and stimulating.

During that period in my life before I "woke up" to the fact that Jesus needed to be "Lord of my life"--I was being influenced by the forces of darkness and didn't even recognize it--several troubling things happened; but He kept blessing and protecting me throughout, waiting patiently for me to wake up. **Ephesians 5:8-10 For you were once darkness, but now you are light in the Lord. Live as children of light (for the fruit of the light consists in all goodness, righteousness and truth) and find out what pleases the Lord.**

Ephesians 5:11,12 Have nothing to do

with the fruitless deeds of darkness, but rather expose them, for it is shameful even to mention what the disobedient do in secret.

Ephesians 5:14 Wake up, O sleeper, rise from the dead, and Christ will shine on you.

Gerald decided to supplement his undergraduate degree with courses to obtain a teachers' certificate. Because the University of Florida had the courses he needed, and because his sister lived in Miami, we decided to move to Miami and apply for college housing. Our first child, Mark, was born while we were staying with his sister, Jackie, an RN, who made sure I stayed healthy. He was a $9^{1/2}$ pound Hercules baby--strong and chubby. When he finally had some real hair instead of peach fuzz, it was almost platinum, a real "tow-head." His exotic turquoise eyes and brown skin (we spent any spare time at the beach) drew much attention wherever we went.

We obtained college housing, and while Gerald studied,took care of Mark, cooked, and passed the required courses, I taught Girls' Physical Education at Shenandoah Junior High School to support the family... enjoyed the students, the activities, my son and husband immensely...only one important element was missing-- not one thought was given to our Lord who provided the wonderful blessings we were receiving. Thanks be to God for being patient and merciful.

Exodus 34:6-7 The Lord, the Lord God, merciful and gracious, long- suffering, and abounding in goodness

and truth, keeping mercy for thousands, forgiving iniquity and transgression and sin...NKJV

To fully trust or appreciate God, one must understand that He is a merciful God, full of compassion and love for His creation. Those who reject the free gift of salvation from His Son, or who take note only of His acts of judgment, can never truly understand God. (from [7]THE POPULAR ENCYCLOPEDIA OF BIBLE PROPHECY, by Tim LaHaye and Ed Hindson.)

This is God, OUR GOD, full of mercy, who always keeps His promises!

Teaching Overseas:

Inagua, Bahamas, and our summer trip to Haiti

Our first tour overseas was to an Island called Inagua, the Southernmost Island in the Bahamas.

At the end of our first school year on Inagua, the Summer of 1961, we decided to hop an Island boat (only about 35 ft. long) that went straight from Inagua to Haiti, thereby avoiding the necessity to travel (by Island boat much bigger than 35 ft. long) all the way North to Nassau, where one had to go to catch a plane to anywhere. Our goal was to spend a month in Haiti, renting a home there (cost of living about half of what it would be in the states), and be able to learn more about the country of some of the friends we had made the past year. (Morton Salt Co. had hired their manager of the Inagua office from Haiti.)

No one had mentioned to us that the little Island boat was pretty primitive (well, they might have mentioned it; but, we were young and adventuresome, and actually thought they were exaggerating—they weren't!) If I hadn't been pregnant with our second child, I don't think the exhaust from the chugging motor would have bothered me; however, our "stateroom," a little nook with a narrow cot tucked in behind the engine room, was the only place for a female to stay safe, unless I wanted to squeeze in up on deck where the "sailors" were frantically trying to keep the water from swamping the boat, while we were going through the place where two seas meet and change directions, the currents roiling the water enough to make the little boat pitch and heave unmercifully. (No wonder very few people chose to take this short cut to Haiti from the Bahamian Islands.)

In between being nauseous and throwing up, I was praying fervently, more sincerely than I had ever done before. I was sure the boat would turn over, and I would be trapped in that wretched little cubicle. All of the sudden, the seas were flat calm...and two hours later, we arrived at Port-Au-Prince. Did I remember to thank Him for answering my prayers? No, at that time, I hadn't realized that God controlled everything and could even stop the roiling sea. I just thought we had finally made it through the rough part.

That was the only boat trip where I was seasick, and I often wonder if the smoky fumes from that grimy engine caused Heidi to be my only child who had childhood asthma. It's something to ponder. Thank the Lord, she eventually grew out of it. Also, She was the only one of my children who had colic for the first three months of her life; however, I blamed that on my selfishness of not stopping smoking while carrying her, even though only a few cigarettes a day. (Later, while teaching Health Education in the Lab. School at the University of Northern Colorado, in Greeley, Colorado, I quit "cold turkey" when I used a model of charred lungs in my classroom...never smoked another cigarette!)

My Dad came down to visit us while we were spending that month in Haiti...we had been able to rent a huge home up on the side of a steep hill where we had a panoramic view of the harbor. After taking a tourist's snapshot of "Papa Doc's extensive Personal Guard" through the spikes of the fence around his Palace, several plainclothes men with pistols stuck into their belts (deliberately in plain view) jumped out of a passing car and demanded my Dad's camera. My Dad said, "No!" They grabbed it out of his hands and walked back to their stopped car, got in, and left.

Even though it was an inexpensive small "Brownie" camera, my Dad was very offended by their threatening manner and decided to leave for home.(two days early) He had been "kinda" understanding when the peasants (colorfully dressed gals with tall pots balanced on their heads carrying water for a long distance, or a man in scraps of colorful pantaloons and white shirt on a burro) he photographed had come to him and demanded payment for being the subject of his photo (they were poor and he felt they needed some means to get a few coins to feed their families); however, after the scare from the government thugs, He was right when he said, "This place gives me the heeby, jeebies!" which in the olden days was a phrase used to mean "the creeps." Today, it means "creepy," or "weird"--something scary in the air.

Back then, Haiti was controlled by a dictator, "Papa Doc" who had turned his back on God (my hindsight) and chosen to embrace the powers of darkness (the voodoo priests), and allowed his people to be controlled by superstition and fear...for his own love of power and money. Most of the people were very poor and afraid to resist the "jefe" (chief) and his republican guard (plain old assassins). My word (chief) should be said in French as the language on the Island is French based, but is more of a combination... like a Creole dialect.

But, being comfortable and well-fed, on a hill above the poverty and undernourished humanity, it was beyond my spiritual maturity at that time to see where the country of Haiti was headed.

Many years later and several dictators later, after the huge earthquake hit and millions were killed and made homeless, my first thought was..."God's wrath!"

My second thought is 2nd Chronicles 7:14 If my people who are called by my name will humble themselves, pray and seek my face, and turn from their wicked ways, then will I hear from heaven, forgive their sins, and heal their land. All of God's people know that God allowed these leaders of our country to be elected, most likely because of our country's continuing and escalating corruption and Idol-worshiping (love of money and material "things" before their love of God.) And, unless the leaders try to cause us to disobey God, we are to give them our allegiance and prayers--especially prayers. If we see, however, that the dictator, oops! I mean the President is turning his back on God...(and chooses to embrace the powers of darkness) and is allowing his people to be controlled by superstition and fear...it is our God-given righteousness to oppose these wrong decisions.

What we should be doing constantly for our country is corporately praying for redemption and revival; if those in control of our country are incurring God's wrath by compromising His precepts about Israel (forcing the division of Jerusalem), with their constant ignoring of our Constitution-- written by His order when the American people revered God and gave Him first place-- and placing the U.S. in jeopardy by siding with Israel's enemies, we need to stand up in God's power for righteousness.

There is some question as to who actually wrote these

remarks years ago, but when I first heard them, they were attributed to Alexis de Toqueville. Supposedly, he said many years ago on a tour of the then mostly agricultural country and after visiting the churches, "**America is great because she is good, and if America ever ceases to be good, America will cease to be great." He also wrote,** "The American Republic will endure until the day Congress discovers that it can bribe the public with the public's money." (Stimulus plan)*My parenthetical addition.*

Whether de Toqueville said those words or not, both remarks have proven to have happened big time. We need to pray unceasingly for our country.

After the Summer trip to Haiti, we began our

second school year on the Island of Inagua;

needless to state, we took a conventional mode of transportation back to the Island:

Our first daughter, Heidi, tiny, (6.4 lbs....thick black hair, wisping around her adorable blue-eyed piquant face) was born on that Island--where we taught for two years in a Bahamian elementary school--Gerald teaching grades five and six; and I, grades three and four. At this time, I found my blood type is O-RH Negative, which meant the Lord had to have been with me when Mark was born, because the hospital in Miami did not require me to have the monthly check for anti-bodies building in my blood against Gerald's positive blood type. In fact, they didn't even have my correct blood type on my papers, which could have been crucial, had I ever needed a blood transfusion.

At any rate, "He Was There All the Time." It only came clear to me in stages, as the scales fell away.

The single Doctor on the island faithfully drew the necessary amount of blood, (on the day the plane flew in), put it in a cooler, and rushed it to the plane just before it took off. Praise God, I never developed the anti-bodies, and Heidi arrived "safe and sound" in the little one room clinic, delivered by the American Doctor on the Island for the employees of the Morton Salt Company. We had been hired by the Bahamian Government, which at that time was still under the auspices of the British.

You see, our Lord has a sense of humor with His compassion...who would have thought a Bahamian employee would need an American Doctor, who was there for the employees of the American company—the Morton Salt Company—who harvested salt from the sea in pans on the southside of the island—to draw blood every month and then to deliver her baby when it was time. It is amazing how He takes care of us when we think we are doing it ourselves!

Gerald decided after two years on Inagua, we needed to head for Europe--specifically Rome—where he had always wanted to go for most of his life. We had saved some money over the two years on the Island; however, without jobs in the near future, our trip to Rome was completely unrealistic-- with two small children—a baby and a toddler-- before the time of disposable diapers and universal washing machines and dryers.(Gerald had promised that we could hire a maid for a pittance in Rome to baby-sit and wash diapers; ironically, the weeks we were there, most of the maids had gone to the mountains with their employers because of the unusual heat. So our two weeks in Rome were in a hotel room with Gerald taking several excursions to see some of Rome...we did take the kids to visit St. Peter's Cathedral, and saw the fountains from the movie, THREE COINS IN THE FOUNTAIN.)

Rome was an experience I could have done without (at that particular time), but survived. We ran out of money, so Gerald deposited us across the Mediterranean in a local (not for tourists) close-to-the beach pensione (very small bed and breakfast Inn) in Spain (when Spain was still relatively inexpensive), and he took a ship home on what we had left—to borrow money enough to send us tickets to come home. Needless to state, that month on the beach in an obscure village in Spain was not a luxurious vacation time. With very little money, much diaper washing, an abandoned lost feeling, and concern that Gerald might go into Mr. Hyde mode and forget about us in a foreign country with no money, the Holy Spirit began to nudge me again (hindsight) to put my faith in Christ Jesus and pray. After that, I felt less abandoned--He did give me peace--and several of the town folk began to be friendly and coo over Mark and Heidi; and even though I didn't know much Spanish, little children encourage communication without words, especially a little "Rubio" (white blonde) toddler, and black-haired, blue-eyed baby girl. Had I truly trusted Him (Jesus) at that time, the experience would have been positive and memorable.

Eventually, Gerald did obtain money for our tickets and wired enough for us to fly home; somehow I gathered our two little ones together, leaving most "things" behind, being too bulky for me to handle with the children, (and I had traded some of them for goat's milk, crackers and cheese) made it to the airport in Barcelona...I, who had always left the travel details to Gerald. My memory about it is nil, so it must have been quite a difficult journey; my skill of blocking out unpleasant happenings is a defense mechanism developed from the "Mr. Hyde" times; plus a lack of confidence at that time, not having Jesus as my Savior and Lord.

San Bernardino, California

Fortunately, after driving and camping across Southern U.S. from Florida to California, there was an opening at San Bernardino High School for a Girls' Physical Education teacher...the large classes were a challenge, especially Archery; but, surprisingly,the students were co-operative and very willing to help. Evidently, the word went around from one of the leaders in the school that the new "gym" teacher was "O.K" because my classes (sometimes 40 -50 girls) were running smoothly while others were having much trouble (probably because most of the girls liked P.E. at that time--the academic classes weremuch too large, very difficult for those with poor reading skills, with homework anddistracting boys in the classes--besides many of the leaders in the school were jockeying for position--the "have nots" resenting the "haves" and vice-versa; and gangs were emerging.)

Thankfully, He was looking after us...because by that time, I was becoming aware that I needed to pray "unceasingly" and trust in Him. We had found a resident motel with one little home in the back with grass and trees; and, a couple who befriended us—an ex-navy man and his Japanese war bride. Kumikogrew to love my small children and graciously agreed to not only keep my two with her own two little girls, but even kept our little house clean for a nominal amount per week. (God sent this little Japanese angel to watch over my children as if they were her own.) Gerald had found a job working for some company selling something, and was gone three or four days per week; but, was itching to go back to teaching...actually, itching to go back overseas.

Lanzarote, Canary Islands

After a year in San Bernardino, California, we once more ventured overseas to New Delhi, India, for two years; then, a year in New York State...and, on to Lanzarote, the southernmost island in the Canary Islands, to start a private school for a combined family of 11 children, ages five to sixteen. (We later found the "Mother" of that huge family was an heiress of, at that time, Mobile Oil Co., and had taken her five children from their Texas home to join with the "Father" of another family whose Dad had kidnapped his own six children from their Mother, who was the legal guardian of his children. We didn't know this until well into the teaching year when we pieced together the stories the children wrote during their English classes).

Gerald became the "Headmaster" and taught grades Six-twelve, sometimes having one student in each class, at the most two. My classes, grades pre-kindergarten through fifth grade had the same, sometimes one, maybe two.

Ursula, our second daughter was born there...an 8½ pound sweetheart...bald, blue-eyed baby girl, announcing her entry into this world with a loud "cry" on the way out.

The main thing I remember about that old castle-hospital maternity ward(?) was the freezing cold, and the bubbling of a sterile(?) pot on a little two-burner heater resting on the floor in the corner of the sparsely furnished room.

Oh, yes! I also remember the old midwife shoving the "Doctor" aside when he didn't seem to know what to do.Later, I found out that MDs do not deliver babies in most of Spain--at least back then--and especially on this Island because they were still in the dark ages (not too much of an exaggeration). Gerald had insisted the Doctor be there...the Doctor at least guaranteed a room in the hospital.(Needless to state, there were no elevators, but some curving stone steps up to a remote room in a tower—I wondered if I would get to the roombefore Ursula was born).

On the Island of Lanzarote, most babies were born at home and were to be born quietly—I suppose to spare males the hard facts of life--thus, there was no actual maternity ward in the hospital. Thank the Lord, Gerald stayed there with me in that scary room; we took Ursula home the next morning.

Again, God is so good...several months later, developing Mastitis, the midwife was able to massage the hardened milk to the surface and lance the infection out of my breasts. Had I been more aware, then, that prayer to Our Father is more effective than trying to be independent and strong within "myself," I would have consulted Him and listened to His messenger (the Midwife) when she told me to wrap firmly, so the milk would stop flowing when I decided to wean Ursula. The midwife had offered to help me..."I can do this myself," was my thought, still not trusting those "old-fashioned" remedies...and ended in much pain and with an unsatisfied baby besides...she didn't like the goat's milk and I would let her nurse some to stop her crying...thereby producing more milk, but not using all of it.

That was one instance when the Lord intervened and healed me when I gave another "emergency" prayer. Did I begin to realize I needed to depend on Him completely instead of "self?" I think I was receiving a glimmer of "Light" at that time.

DYING TO SELF

Despite every adversity, heartache and problem, Jonathon had declared time and again, "the Lord hath buttered my steps." With each new experience and step forward in the ministry and desire to bring the love and beauty of Jesus to suffering, perishing nations, Jonathon declared, "I die a thousand deaths and was continuously cast upon that incredible promise of God that I would die in the east of my land. I came to the realization of what death really is: "Oh, it's so easy to say the "cross," declared Jonathon, "but what did it really mean? As I died, I SAW THAT THE HOLY SPIRIT WAS WORKING WITHIN TO CRUCIFY EVERY AMBITION AND DESIRE THAT IS CONTRARY TO HIS NATURE AND WILL. Ambition and self was exposed and rooted out. THE GREAT CONCERN OF THE HOLY SPIRIT IS WITH THE MOTIVES OF OUR HEARTS and HE IS CONTINUALLY EXAMINING THEM TO REPLACE THE CORRUPT NATURE OF SELF WITH THE CHARACTER OF JESUS." (my caps)... from the book, [1]RECKLESSLY ABANDONED, by Michael Howard.

When I read Michael Howard's book, I knew the Lord had brought it to my attention for the purpose of reading that one paragraph; however, I marveled throughout the book at Jonathon's (probably Michael Howard, as this was a true story) trust and faith in Jesus Christ, our Lord. With his life in danger at every turn, he followed that still, small voice (once, quite urgent)) immediately and completely, not letting anything distract him from his obedience, saving his physical life many times. Spiritually, although he was sold out to the Lord, he still had to "die to self"

51

many times just as any true Christian does because of the "Deceiver" trying anew every day to invade by using our "self" indulgences as bait.

Yet, having heard all of these phrases..."die to self", "love the lord, thy God, with all of your heart, mind, and strength", "put God first, then all good things will follow"...most of my life, none of them registered into my sub-conscious self because I was much too busy pleasing "Number one--"self" as the world was propagandizing, beginning in the sixties, carrying on through the seventies and even worse today as criminals are given passes even though they take what they want, impervious to laws. That's what happens when we take God out of schools, public life, and even churches.

My praise for the Lord is constant now that He chose to wake me up and shake up the self-absorbent trance I was in for many years of my life. This book, hopefully, might help several others realize the futility of concentrating on self-satisfaction...oh, it is very difficult to break a life-long habit, but it can be done with Jesus...much prayer... and much time in THE WORD. And, every day a renewal of your prayer, "Lord, let me concentrate on doing things for Your glory, and please keep Satan behind me in your precious Name!"

Wake-up Call

When I needed wakeup, God used failing health to break my "close-mindedness." Truly, my real awakening came when nothing would heal my bad feet. Having been full of good health all of my teaching years, then moving to Hobbs because of Jack's stroke, developing planter fascia first and painful aching tops of my feet up to the ankle, all I could think of was getting my feet back to normal.

The breakthrough finally came after five-and-one-half years when I was surfing the channels and ended on GLC (God's Learning Channel) and heard Dr. Scott say, "I had neuropathy in my feet three years ago; but have it no longer." That caught my attention! I had already given up on steroid shots into the nerves of my feet...the treatment was more painful than the cure; it really wasn't a cure, only temporary relief; so, I was desperate!

When I found God's Learning Channel, I re-established God's purpose in my life, or I should say, I finally zeroed in on it--internalized it if you will. My purpose in this world is not only to tell others about Jesus; but it is to write this book to help me and other "Christians" wake up to the fact that God does have a purpose for us all and will make it apparent to us when we give our whole self to Jesus.

"This was the kind of life Jonathan wanted to live. To be cast upon the God he so desperately loved; believing, trusting, and knowing that He is able in every circumstance. All God needed were men and women who would be big enough to believe Him...'It's for me,'

he shouted, 'for me!'" from [1]RECKLESSLY ABANDONED by Michael Howard

The Lord has shown me that Spirit (if only we had known then that, with Jesus, we could have banished the demon Mr. Hyde)--believing and walking with Him in complete obedience has allowed me to claim His promises found in Matthew 10:1,7,8 for keeping us healthy to work in and for the Kingdom...which soon will be " the New Jerusalem."

He called his twelve disciples to him and gave them authority to drive out evil spirits and to heal every disease and sickness. Matthew 10:1

As you go, preach this message: "The kingdom of heaven is near. Heal the sick, raise the dead, cleanse those who have leprosy, drive out demons. Freely you have received, freely give. Matthew 10:7-8

If we are not obedient to God's will and commandments, though, and deliberately repeat sin for which we have already been forgiven, eventually, He does take His protection from us and will not hear our prayers for good health when we try to claim His promises about good health. In fact, several Bible verses warn us what His promises are if we continue in our sinful ways. Here is one:

Micah 6:13 Therefore I will also make you sick by striking you, by making you desolate because of your sins.

Are you looking for your purpose? If we want to fulfill it before Jesus comes, which the signs say are not too far off, we have to repent of our sins, study the Bible, and "hear" the WORD...then, we'll find our purpose.

HE WILL KEEP HIS PROMISES! (IF we are in His will.)

New Delhi, India

Having taught in New Delhi, India, for two years soon after Heidi was born, the Superintendent invited us to come back for another two-year contract when Ursula was about two years old. The second time we went to New Delhi, the school's name had been changed from The American International School to The American School, evidently because of International politics.

Gerald found a friend, an Indian journalist, who kept him informed about Indira Gandhi's policies (She was the Prime Minister of India at the time.) Gerald was in his element to know the news before it appeared in the newspaper; and, he felt as if he might have been making history by sharing any tidbits of rumors (colored with his opinions) that he heard floating around the school or the American community.

The school wasn't too happy about his getting involved in Indian politics, however, because at that time, some very sensitive negotiations were going on "behind the scene." Therefore, "Mr. Hyde's" contract was not renewed for the second year at the school because of his rebellion against the American School's re-organization under the umbrella of the A.I.D... an agency of the USA.

Gerald and I had enjoyed having students not only from India, but also from Europe (Poland, Hungary...at that time, still behind the "iron curtain"), China, Afghanistan, the Kashmir, and many others...mostly sons and daughters of the Ambassadors from those countries. With the reorganization, however, all other students besides American, were no longer eligible to attend The American School. I never understood why. But, I knew why Mr. Hyde was becoming dominant...

Katrina, my third daughter, was born in the midst of this political intrigue, and was a breath of fresh air--7.4 lbs. of wriggling, talc-smelling cuteness--a salvation for my sanity of dealing with his "Mr. Hyde's" personality almost constantly--because of the meetings in our house where gin was flowing freely.

After another year of trying to persuade Gerald to use our ticket home, my ultimatum finally worked when even his Indian friends deserted him because of his "Mr. Hyde's" treatment of his wife and new baby. Those were the years when my love for "Dr. Jekyll" was tried beyond repair, and after returning stateside, when his "Mr. Hyde" personality was coming to the fore, I had to leave the older children sleeping, grab Katrina and leave for our designated hiding place for the night, until early morning when he had fallen into a drunken stupor.

Single Mother

When Mark had graduated from Maxwell High School, and joined the Air Force, "Mr. Hyde" was committed to the Las Vegas, NM, State Hospital. Having been an "enabler" long enough, I filed for a "Restraining Order" and a separation from my husband of almost 20 years. By that time, I was beginning to realize that hole in my heart was growing and I just didn't know how to fill it. I had four beautiful, healthy children for whom I was very thankful and loved very much; but, being a single Mother had not been on my agenda. Thinking my marriage was for life, and having taken no college courses for raising three daughters on my own (a helpless feeling), my thoughts were muddled; but, we actually did fine (I convinced myself) and grew closer to each other without the constant bickering, broken promises, and derision coming from "Mr. Hyde."

My absolute certainty at that time was to never marry again and to be "footloose and fancy free." TheWomen's Lib. groups were dominating the media and were able to influence any disillusionedwoman/girl who was not strong in her "faith" in Jesus. I had a very wrong idea about life and marriage at that time... never having read Solomon's Song of Songs, which many say is "a love poem about a real human love relationship, and that all loving, committed marriages are reflections of God's love."

A simple poem I wrote to my 18 yr. old Granddaughter about a month after my second husband, John "Jack" C. Briggs passed away indicates why I finally decided to marry again 30 years ago.

THANK YOU, LORD!

Thank you, Lord for giving me Jack!
He was your instrument to get me on track.
The way to YOU is narrow and straight...
Not veering off left and tempting fate.
When you're young and really think you're somethin'...
You're full of self, but truly don't know nothin'
"Sowing wild oats" is the excuse we give...
We know perfectly well that is no way to live.
The consequences today for living your own way...
Can be forever...Satan will make you pay.
Time is getting short to make up your mind;
to straighten up your act and go looking to find...
A way to live without one foot in the world;
It's all or nothing with JESUS, the Bible unfurled. (opened up)
Put HIM first in all...you'll no longer be uncertain...
Though there's no guarantee you'll never be hurtin'...
On HIS path you'll stride with confidence and love...
No "hate crime" will touch you, 'cause HIS grace from above...
Will go with you forever and ever that's sure...
HIS promises will sooth you and always endure.
THANK YOU, LORD! ...From Grandma Carol

Praise God for sending Maj. John C. "Jack" Briggs, Ret., into my life (some 30 yrs. Ago) before I had made too many wrong decisions, not only about my "love life," but also about my permissiveness with my teen-age daughters.

Once I felt ex-communicated from my obligation (to raise my children in the Catholic Church) because of the divorce, I returned to the Bible-preaching church of my early years, where Jack and I went together every service and Bible study. Jack presented me with a Good News Bible soon after we were married. It was a very good translation in which to begin, because I seemed to actually understand what I was reading. The next Bible he gave me was the New King James Version, and as I slowly became more grounded in the Word, Jesus answered my prayers and filled me with the Holy Spirit at my request; therefore I was realizing He was already in me and had been guiding me all those years when I thought it was "my conscience" doing the guiding.

He answers Prayer

The "knowledge" doesn't come to you by osmosis...it comes through hearing the Word, reading and cross-referencing scripture, and constant prayer. His promise is He will give us an answer IF we ask...it may not be the answer we want, but, He knows what we need; therefore, the answer will be according to our needs...which may be no answer at all until another time. That's another great thing about the Lord, our Lord...His timing is perfect.

When God decided to move us to Hobbs from Quemado (where Jack's dream had been realized...140 acres, plus building his own cabin, plus being able to ride his fences on his own horses), needless to state, Jack protested some; however, having just had a stroke in February of 2003, he was not as assertive and decisive as he had been throughout most of our marriage...and I believe he was realizing at last that he wasn't immortal, and that he probably could not take care of finishing the other two sections of the cabin, feeding, watering and exercising four horses every day, fixing fence, driving 35 miles to pick up hay and grain when we needed it...even with God's help...after all, at 85 years of age at that time, he "could have handled it"...And he might have...

But, the stroke was a wakeup call for us both and even though I was 17 years younger than he, he was of a frame of mind where he never felt any older than about 40.

At any rate, (after much prayer) the Lord smoothed the way for us to find a comfortable home in Hobbs and to sell our property in Quemadofor cash, evidently because we had prayed for His will to be done and He had indicated that we needed to be closer to medical facilities and to family. (For many years I had prayed that my son and daughters' families would settle in a place where they would be surrounded by Christians...and would become a part of the Family of God. HE answered my prayers. Heidi, my first daughter, and Dan, her husband, live in Las Cruces, NM, where their children attend a Christian school and are inundated with Christian principles...hopefully have their own quiet time in the Word. My son and family and two other daughters and families are in Hobbs).

People were asking me, "How did you know that was His will?" The neat thing about God, our God, is He lets you know His will in many different ways; therefore, you need to know Him and His character in order to discern His will. The only way to do that is to immerse yourself in the Bible, Christian books that are telling about how God's character was revealed to them, and GLC (God's Learning Channel)-- where you will HEAR the Word. Compare your Pastor's interpretation of the Word with the previous mentioned, and your own understanding when you pray before you read the same scripture.Then, as many have indicated, He will open doors of opportunity to follow His will, and slam the doors shut if it comes from another source, like one of those little temptations provided by him who knows our weaknesses, and who is waiting impatiently in the wings to take center stage in drawing you away from our Lord. Every day it is necessary to pray in Jesus' name to keep Satan behind you, 'cause his main purpose in life is to be in charge and to steer you away from God, our God, one way or another.

Quemado, NM

Let me relate my first realization that angels are here for us...which finally dawned on me when we lived in Quemado, NM. Many times I had read Christian and non-Christian books about angels appearing when people needed God most...often in the form of a stranger whom they never saw again after the need was alleviated. When I read the fiction and non-fiction stories about angels, I tended to lump them all together as just interesting tales... until I began to read the Bible and pray more and discuss more and really think about and digest and memorize key scriptures suggested by my dedicated Christian friends.

Our trumpet- playing Pastor in Quemado at the time, Tom Pieper, asked who would like to be a part of a Bible study called EXPERIENCING GOD three hours each Thursday evening for 12 weeks. I hesitated...because as it was, teaching five days a week, grading papers and making lesson plans most evenings, refereeing volleyball most weekends (Friday or Saturday evenings), Jack didn't see me much. Although he always accompanied me to church and Sunday school, in-depth Bible studies didn't seem to be his "cup-o-tea"...as he put it. I had avoided committing that much time for an actual Bible course, with homework and all. Remembering that my required summer courses to keep up my teaching certificate were finally over, (as I had only a few years to retirement...nine to be exact); did taking on another "obligation" seem desirable to my hectic life of using every spare hour of daylight helping Jack add another log to our almost-finished first-section of our log cabin?

Our Lord made the decision for me...sending me to the first meeting of the class at Bonnie Armstrong's house. The first week's lesson was so captivating, I couldn't wait for the next week...someone must have prayed me into that study...most likely Elsie Candelaria...my Mentor...and probably one of my Guardian Angels. Looking back, that Bible study marked my first heart-mind knowledge that I needed to have a closer, more intimate relationship with my Savior, our Savior, and that I should look to see where God, our God, is working...then make myself available and join Him in His work.

So when Lynn, my teacher friend and "Angel" invited me to assist her in starting a GA (Girls in Action) at the church, my first response was "Yes!" because I knew from teaching these girls at school that they needed an activity after school where they would be encouraged to help others. While working with those pre-teenage little girls, memorizing scriptures and doing crafts using the scriptures, I found they began to get through to my innermost being —especially when we sang praise songs with words from scripture. The prayer circle at the end of our session became a favorite with the girls because they could give prayer requests and then pray for that person out-loud when it was their turn. I thank God for Lynn and her deep faith being the example I dearly needed at that particular time for a more genuine relationship with Jesus; and showing those little gals that Jesus is there for them.

Joan and Bernice, two special friends in Elsie's Sunday school class with me, were such good examples of absolute faith and Christian love...they were another reason my faith grew in leaps and bounds those 13 years we were in Quemado. Lou Brown, our second Pastor Doug Brown's wife, personified the love of Jesus, and with her Bible studies for the women of the church, we were truly blessed every time we came together in Jesus' name.

About that time, I read the true story, CHRISTIE, by Catherine Marshall; then, A MAN CALLED PETER. Eye-openers! What a writer she was!...God-inspired I'm sure. Praise the Lord, our Lord, for inundating me with Godly people, Godly books, and a real hunger for God's Word... Jesus Christ. Why did it take so long for me to finally rid myself of those on-again, off-again "scales"...one minute my eyes were open to the truth...then, the next, bogged down again with the "wiles of the world"...

Why? God's Plan...

Being brought up with the "work- to-get-ahead" ethic, and not much prayer in our household, plus a large, beautiful family Bible, brought out only when necessary to record births and deaths, my thoughts about God, our God, were mostly as a distant Benevolent Benefactor when I really wanted something badly; so would pray and bargain with God; or a stern Disciplinarian if my behavior was bad...kind of like a Father I didn't want to disappoint. But, most of the time, I was so busy being busy, my thoughts never considered much of anything other than the present activity and how I could look good to people I wanted to impress.

And, then, of course, straight-from-the-devil ads on TV starting back in the 60s-80s..."Look out for number one" plus, "Do anything you please, as long as it doesn't hurt anyone else." Then, in the nineties..."Do whatever feels good to you." ... And, "Take that vacation--you deserve it", and, all of these slogans that promote yourself first... not God, our God.

Straight out of the "Deceiver's" handbook, and probably one of his most effective tools for causing us to have scales over our eyes and earplugs in our ears when Jesus is trying to communicate with us.

I didn't know God's Word; so, I was easily convinced that one had to take care of No. One (yourself) because nobody else would...what an appealing slogan that was/is to insecure teen-agers or young adults and many grown-ups who haven't yet realized that they need Jesus. Perhaps you see yourself in some of these instances I'm writing about. Believe me, my story is probably fairly typical of kids who grew up in those times; but, if you found the Lord, our Lord, no matter what age, I know you feel as fortunate as I that He chose you.

By this time, you are probably saying to yourself, "What does all this have to do with preparing for the New Jerusalem? " My thanks be to God, our God, every morning, noon, and night, that I have been being groomed for this job while still in the womb; to tell every person who crosses my path about Jesus. And, if you love Him and obey Him, you will want to tell everyone about Him!

Yes, I believe every experience, no matter how innocuous, has been in my life so I could tell you just how much we are loved by our Savior and Lord, Prince of Peace, omnipresent, omniscient, and desiring of our love in return. He wants everyone to embrace this belief and turn away from purely pleasing themselves, which is how Satan operates.

But, I'm digressing. On with the illumination...which in the cartoon world, a light bulb appears above one's head when one finally "gets it."

Now that you understand that I'm a firm believer in God's, our God's, provision for our protection as well as our spiritual well-being, you might as well get it with "both barrels." I truly believe that everything happens according to God's plan; even the little details that make up our daily lives...nothing is too trivial for God's, our God's, attention. Once this becomes internalized, (part of our thinking), then you can truly make yourself available for God (Adonai), our God, to do His work in a mighty way, sometimes through you...*IF you are truly saturated with Jesus and are obedient to His will.*

*In the Bible, God, our Go*d, oftentimes used unbelievers to punish His people when they had turned away from Him to the idols of the world. Unless those unbelievers found the Light, however, they were/are eventually "judged" for their transgressions against "Israel" (Israel includes us believers as well; we are grafted onto the "Tree of Life" because of our unfailing love for and obedience to the Will of God, our God; and because we have seen the "light," we are supposed to be a "light" for those Hebrews and/or anyone who hasn't accepted Jesus as their Messiah--)

Genesis 12:3 "I will bless those who bless you, and I will curse him who curses you; And in you all the families of the earth shall be blessed."

A different outlook begins to permeate our whole being; and many of the world's happenings seem to roll off our back, not even soaking into our consciousness, which is focusing on our conversations with Jesus, who becomes more precious to us as we fall more and more in love with Him.

When I finally realized He was smoothing the way for me to go to Israel, I became more and more aware of a hungering for more information on anything about Jerusalem. Somehow, (not coincidence) the New Jerusalem, mentioned in Revelation, caught my attention; and, one day, He woke me early (about 4:30 a.m.), indicated I needed to go to the computer and type this title: PREPARING FOR THE NEW JERUSALEM.

That was in October,about six weeks before my trip. In

that context, my visit to the Holy City rounded out my previous yearnings and satisfied a need to "walk where Jesus walked." (Now, I can tell about how those yearnings were magnified).

MY TRIP TO ISRAEL:

Having traveled much of my earlier years teaching school around the globe, it was my inclination to remain stateside for the remainder of my years...fulfilling any tasks My Lord Jesus Christ directed me to do in order to further His Kingdom.

Isn't God good? Being a "late bloomer" in concentrating onGod's Will, He encouraged me to take one last excursion... into the realm of His Holy Land...not only for elucidation and revelation, but He has accorded me the privilege of seeing "first-hand" Jerusalem as it is today... as a pre-curser for our eternal promise of The New Jerusalem.

Actually, about three months ago, (August '09) I had no inkling that I would ever cross the ocean again...especially into the Middle East where the unrest is obvious and the "principalities of darkness" are throwing everything they have in their bags of discontentment... as a last -ditch effort to wipe the people chosen by God off the face of the earth. Needless to state, (while watching God's Learning Channel), when I heard Tommie say there were several places available in the November 30th tour, my mind hardly registered the fact...or so I thought. The "fact" kept popping up in my mind at the oddest times.

To make a long story short, after viewing several GLC

programs that seemed to refer and stress those openings in the tour...my message seemed to be..."go for it!"

With every hurdle easily cleared, (birth certificate copy expedited by Katrina, my daughter, who can get anything done on the computer)(up-to-date passport forthcoming) (IRA comingdue and necessary to take out...just enough to pay for my tripwith a little spending money besides)... God had arranged everything...including my confidence that, with Him, we need fear no missile attacks, suicide bombers, or anythingthe "enemy" might try to do to harm God's people (that's us).

So, armed with a pen and a journal, this story/adventure will continue...

Happily, the Lord chose the GLC tour for me...whose leaders have many trips behind them and have their sites chosen for the best way for me to experience all that the Lord has waiting for me. Tommie expressed it best... she wrote, "Go expecting God to meet you there and to reveal more of Himself to you than ever before."

She also said, "Pray for our trip, so that it will be a blessing to all of us and to the people of Israel."

My first thought about the trip was to ask our Lord for His blessings on all of us...50 all together.

When my daughter deposited me at the Midland-Odessa airport, she didn't stay...as it was quite early in the morning and she had to get back to Hobbs for work at 8:00.

ISRAEL HERE I COME!

My first encounter with a fellow traveler was very typical of God's provision of guardian angels. She even had silver-platinum hair and an ethereal glow about her face. She must have noticed a strained look about my face, or being a guardian angel, instinctively knew that I needed a boost and a helping hand...or two.

Having read in the GLC info that we could take sox, soap, and razors (throw-away) to the Barrack Brigade, it had not crossed my mind that bar soap is quite solid and the ten bars wrapped in ten pair of sox were very heavy. I was sitting there ruing the day that I hadn't sent them back home with Katrina...when my lovely angel, Denise, came over to introduce herself...my frantic eye contact with hers probably touched her philanthropic nature. She explained that she had flown many times (I checked her back, but didn't see any feathers...PUN-- angel, wings, feathers...get it) and knew how to distribute weight so most of it would be in the checked bag. I didn't ask her how she knew that I needed to switch things around in my bags, (of which I had one too many because of the soapy sox). I figured angels have ESP; she proceeded to open my two carry-ons and one large bag (to be checked), and moved the soap-in-sox into that bag.

Then, I mentioned that I had an extra carry-on bag and maybe I should try to get rid of it somehow. Denise looked around and spotted a lone traveler, a man who had the tour name-tag hanging around his neck. "Gilbert," Denise called walking toward him...how she read his name tag from that distance I'll never know; oh, yes, ESP, I forgot. Whatever she said to him convinced him (since he had only one carry-on) to sling my third bag over his shoulder and to offer introductions, conversation, and a tour-long friendship with Denise and me.

The ice was broken that morning in the Midland-Odessa

airport and every tour member that flew out of that airport had become members of another family--the GLC Israel tour family. The neat thing was our common denominator, Yeshua, tied us together as nothing else could. We flew into Houston where more of our tour group joined us on the flight to Newark, NJ.

The leg of the trip across the ocean to Tel Aviv was somewhat foggy in my mind as most of the time, K.J. (Al and Tommie's daughter) and I were getting to know each other. She had been on this trip before, and was knowledgeable about every technical button and lever, as well as where to put a pillow for long-term sitting, plus pointed out "vacancy" signs front and behind. My assigned seat was next to her... coincidence...No!

As this was my first trip overseas since 1970, God's, our God's, appointments of Denise and K.J. were nothing short of genius. I felt very fortunate as well as sorry for the other "first timers." (However, they probably were assigned Angels also) Thank you, Lord!

Coming in to Tel Aviv, arrival time about 4:15 p.m., our excitement began to build...were we really in Israel? The Holy Land! First timers could hardly believe it., but there was no time to digest it...we had to get our bags, get into the airport, and claim our other bag so it could be loaded onto the bus... to the hotel, pick up our room keys, freshen up, and be at dinner on time (6 P.M.)...so didn't have much time to explore that evening.

After losing about eight hours on the flight over, some experienced "jet lag" big time, and seemed to be a group of sleep-walkers, running on "empty"; but being more energetic than ever, my roommate and I earnestly tried

71

to follow the suggestion that we not go to bed before 10 P.M. or we might wake up around 2:00 A.M. I had met my roommate in Newark, but we didn't have time to talk until we moved into our room at the Renaissance Tel Aviv Hotel. Standing at our window on the tenth floor and looking out at the Mediterranean Sea, both Joyce and I felt as if we needed to pinch ourselves to be sure we were really awake and not dreaming. The view was not only spectacular, it was breathtaking...we were in Tel Aviv...one of the first settlements of the State of Israel... revitalized in the treaty of 1948.

Why had God blessed us so much? Probably for the same reason He does everything...He has a plan and we are all part of it...and blessing His people is one of His pleasures.

Our first dinner on Israeli soil was a gustatory adventure... one had so many choices of so many exotic foods that it numbed our lagging, or should I say our flagging, decision-making process. Remember, we had just missed a night's sleep. However, many of us tried to take a little of everything...but, the plates weren't big enough. Needless to state, the next morning came awfully soon after going to bed sated (full)...or so it seemed.

Obedience

The Israeli people are delightful...they are like most Americans used to be when I was a small child. A small, developing country--they have come a long way in a short time--they have been blessed by God. Nineteen and forty-eight (1948)--62 years--technology equal to any first-world country...He has kept every promise.

However, I am not referring only to physical and technical growth...my amazement is about their communal Spirit for God and their complete regard for each other. Most that I met or observeddisplayed an enthusiasm for "chai"... LIFE...and a concern for each other...and a zest for pleasing others that I haven't seen much lately in the U.S.

What popped into my head early this morning upon awakening (and I'm sure others already discovered this) is that the feasts and Passover and Hanukkah are the glue that melds them together with one aim...to obey God and love Him first ...even before themselves.(Perhaps they have learned much from a stormy history of what happens when one continually disobeys God.)

Many in the U.S. began to serve another when the wily "usurper" (Satan) instilled in the television ads all that was necessary to get ahead was "to serve yourself." "Take care of #1" This progressed into, "Well, if I don't take care of myself, nobody else will"...which progressed into..."Do anything you want to do as long as it doesn't hurt anyone else" to "Do anything you want as long as you get what you want." The latest is "You deserve anything you want!"Some of this kind of behavior was called, "Dog eat Dog" in the business world and in true "trickle down"manner(starting with the executives of organizations), this kind of behavior became the norm rather than the exception...keeping pace with "taking God out of the equation of living."

While Israel was fighting to simply "HAVE" a country, our country was starting to decline into a "me, me me entity." Not a country...but a land of individuals doing what they think is right according to their own desires instead of their Creator's commands and the good of the country.

It is pure "idolatry" to worship "self" and the "sly old fox" is laughing in his sleeve about how successful he has been. Unfortunately, he has made his minions (demons) sly as well, knowing perfectly how to gain control of those people (my first husband and me before we knew Jesus) who want to be indulged consantly (who don't even realize that God is in control and that their destructive behavior will be judged one day.) It seems He is judging all along... arthritis, sugar diabetes, and other adult diseases are fast becoming prevalent in youngsters...could this be because many parents are so in the habit of self-indulgence (except with Jesus), that they are exemplifying this to their offspring...not only in foods, but in "things" (bigger-screen TVs, phones, I-pods, computers, etc.)?

The problem is while his minions control the U.S., their destructive power may destroy our country before God's people wake up and **"humble themselves and pray, seek My Face, and turn from their wicked ways...then I will hear from heaven, forgive them, and heal their land." 2nd Chronicles 7:14**

However, I believe an awakening is happening all over the world...God is restoring His Kingdom...Are we ready and available for Him to use us to help wake up our complacent brothers and sisters as well as to help Him heal the blind, uninformed, and the lost? *Don't miss out on the blessings!*

2ⁿᵈ Chronicles 7:14 (these questions are from Life Action Ministries and used with permission) given to our congregation by Pastor Doug Brown, (whose wife, Lou, was another Angel God sent to wake me up). Ask yourself these questions:

"IF MY PEOPLE..."
1. Am I a child of God?
2. Do I recognize that I am now under "new ownership," that Ihave"been bought with a price" and that I belong to God?
3. Is my relationship with God the most important thing in my life?
"WHO ARE CALLED BY MY NAME..."
1. Do unsaved people in my neighborhood community and workplace know that I'm a Christian?
2. Do I consider it a privilege to be known as a child of God?
3. Do I quickly identify myself as a believer when I come in contact with unbelievers?
4. Do I reflect His holiness and integrity in my daily conduct and dealings with people?
5. When those around me have a personal or spiritual need, do they turn to me to help them find real answers?
"WILL HUMBLE THEMSELVES..."
1. Do I consider others as better than myself?

2. Do I rejoice when others are praised or promoted and I am overlooked?

3. Am I more conscious of my own unworthiness and spiritual poverty than of the faults and failures of those around me?

4. Do I desire to serve those of my family, church, and community, and make them a success?

5. Am I quick to admit when I am wrong and to seek forgiveness?

6. Do I grieve over my sin and how it affects a Holy God?

7. When I'm at odds with someone, do I take the initiative to get it reconciled?

8. Do I take personal responsibility for the condition of my life, rather than blaming circumstances onto others?

9. Do I forgive easily?

"AND PRAY..."

1. Do I pray? Do I spend a set amount of time EVERY DAY in prayer?

2. Do I faithfully pray for the needs of my spouse, children. Grandchildren and other family members?

3. Do I pray regularly for my pastor, church, and other believers?

4. Do I pray earnestly for revival and spiritual awakening in my community?

5. If revival in my home, church, and community depended on my prayers, would there be revival?

"AND SEEK MY FACE..."

1. Do I spend time DAILY at the feet of Jesus, listening to His Word and worshiping Him?

2. Does Jesus occupy the center of my thoughts?

3. Do I earnestly seek to learn all I can about Jesus on a regular basis? (Bible, books, church)

4. Do I look forward to Sunday, so I can go to God's house for worship, fellowship, and instruction?

5. When I face difficult decisions, do I instinctively turn to God for His solution and His wisdom?

"AND TURN FROM THEIR WICKED WAYS..."

1. Do I love righteousness and hate evil?

2. Do I quickly agree with God when He convicts me of sin?

3. Have I confessed all known sin in my life to God?

4. Have I repented and forsaken the sin in my life and asked for His forgiveness?

5. Am I accountable to a godly person for any areas of my life where I may still be vulnerable to return to my "wicked ways?"

"THEN, AND ONLY THEN, WILL I HEAR FROM HEAVEN AND FORGIVE THEIR SIN AND HEAL THEIR LAND."

Back to the Israeli people...by celebrating the festivals together, everyone is worshiping God together. Shabbat, (which means Sabbath) is every Friday evening until Saturday at sundown. Everything is closed up tight...no one thinks of staying open (because they are obeying God.) They do no work on the Sabbath,

...God said "The 7th day is to be a day of rest...a day to contemplate the Goodness of God...to worship and honor Him." Therefore, the Lord blessed the Sabbath Day and made it holy. Exodus 20:11b

How many in our country obey God's directions about the Sabbath?

The Divine Presence has never departed from the Western Wall.

"The Western Wall has been the center of Jewish

yearning and memory for more than 2000 years. The only fragment of the Great Temple to survive the Roman destruction, the Divine Presence has never departed from The Western Wall. Built to support the western side of the Temple Mount, it is known as the Western Wall (in Hebrew, HaKotel HaMa'aravi), it is the most sacred structure of the Jewish people. Its ancient stones stand testimony to a glorious Jewish past, a proud heritage and an extraordinary national rebirth. It is a focus of Jewish longing and prayer for redemption and renewal.

Long before the Temple stood on this mount, Abraham came here to sacrifice his son Isaac (which, if you don't know the story, God provided a ram for the actual sacrifice; but, tested Abraham and reinforced His knowledge of Abraham's obedience...Gen. 22:1-19). Jacob slept here, dreaming of a ladder to heaven (Gen. 22:10-22) Then called Mount Moriah, its summit was where Solomon built the Temple on the land which his father, King David, purchased from Aravnah, the Jebusite, 3,000 years ago. That Temple, destroyed by the Babylonian conqueror Nebuchadnezzar in 586 BC, was rebuilt 70 years later and restored to its original glory by Herod, 2,000 years ago. In 68 CE, this temple was destroyed by the Romans, burned to the ground and its stones scattered with only the Western Wall untouched.

The prophet, Isaiah, called the Temple a "house for all nations." A universal center of spirituality, it stirs the thoughts and emotions of Jew and Non-Jew, and energizes the inner connection between the individual and God. Even with the Temple destroyed, the holiness of the place is such that it remains sacred and, for Jews, central, with every generation facing it in prayer. Today, people from all over the world converge here, to see, feel and pray, and wedge notes, requests and pleas between its timeless stones." (These three paragraphs are word-for-word from a pamphlet distributed to us as we entered the Western Wall Plaza, probably prepared by The Western Wall Heritage Foundation.)

Prayer Requests

Having collected prayer requests from our brothers and sisters in Christ before I left for Israel, my stack of folded requests needed to be placed into several cracks in the Western wall. After doing so, I prayed for all of the requests at once, as I had not opened any of the folded papers... but, Jesus knew every one of them, having been with each one when they wrote them.

When I placed the palm of my hand against the wall, a very noticeable peace came over me...and, I began to back away from the wall as I saw others doing.

Almost in a state of languor, my eyes began to slide upward, coming to a small recess in the wall, where I saw two gray pigeons backed into the opening (what I thought I saw at the time were two gray pigeons and a white dove--but, upon reflection, that small opening couldn't have held three birds, could it?)

As I was looking at the birds and still backing slowly with my counterparts on either side of me, I found myself praying, "Thank you, Lord, for showing me these three birds and answering our prayers"...at that same moment, one of those birds flew straight off its perch toward me, flying lower and lower until I had to duck down to avoid being struck by it.

*I was so amazed, I didn't turn around to see where it went from there; but, I just had a definite assurance that our prayers were answered. I know for sure one was answered because at the same time I was putting the requests in their niches...a member of our congregation who had given me a folded request made it a point to tell me her son had begun to recover from all of his problems on such-and-such a day at a certain time...it was the time I was praying at the wall.**Isn't our God marvelous?***

To Know Our Savior

More and more my mind, spirit, and body are being relinquished to my, our merciful God; and more and more my understanding of the scriptures is allowing me to become a true member of the family of Abraham, Isaac, and Jacob. A wider knowledge of our Jewish roots is a necessity to know our Savior...no wonder He wanted me to go to Jerusalem.

Romans 11:33,36 Oh, the depth of the riches of the wisdom and knowledge of God!

How unsearchable His judgments, and His paths beyond tracing out!

For from Him and through Him and to Him are all things

To Him be the glory forever! Amen

OH, HOW I LOVE JESUS![3]

This is another song which especially touches my heart and has a simple message, but quite profound in its simplicity:

(1) There is a name I love to hear, I love to sing its worth;

It sounds as music to my ear, the sweetest name on earth.

CHORUS: Oh, how I love Jesus, Oh, how I love Jesus,

Oh, how I love Jesus, Because He first loved me.

(2) It tells me of a Savior's love, Who died to set me free;

It tells me of His precious blood, The sinner's perfect plea. (C)

(3) It tells me what my Father has...In store for every
    day;
And though I tread a darksome path, yields sunshine all
    the way. (C)
(4) It tells of One whose loving heart...Can feel my deepest
    woe,
Who in each sorrow bears a part, That none can bear
    below. (C)

If you do attend church and raise up your voice in song
to the Lord, and actually think about the words and the
message of the words, there is no way for you to be
unmoved by the Holy Spirit. (Singing hymns to Jesus was
the first "bleep" in my heart moving me toward Him.)

*True, it is helpful to have a combination of head
knowledge, heart knowledge, and Spiritual knowledge of
the character of our Triune God in order to be worshipful
in your music...but, I've found that comes with a continual
closer relationship with Jesus, my Lord and Savior, every
day in Bible study and prayer.*

(To be prepared for the NEW JERUSALEM, learning about
the character of our "triune" God is very important as well
as to know how much He loves us whether we please Him
or not; however,if we truly love Him, we want to please
Him all the time. That can be done by spending time with
Him in the Word, and by asking the Holy Spirit to fill you,
show you, guide you and "sanctify" (purify) you; and by
singing His hymns with a joyful smile straightfrom the
HEART.)

Every time you sing a hymn like the one above, belting
it out and feeling it deep in your "lower bowels" (an old-
time Biblical term), you are pleasing and coming closer

to Him...and rebuffing the "Enemy." And, showing our Precious Savior how much you love and revere Him. (You are also being a "light" for others to lose their self-consciousness in worshiping our Lord-God.) When you become the "Light" that exemplifies Jesus, your behavior is closely monitored by those around you; they see your joy in Jesus, and that is a witness in itself.

The message of this song is important because people (my "old self" included) are so wrapped up in pleasing themselves that they never actually "see" (or hear about) Jesus...their hearts have been hardened from their worldly pursuits and satisfying impulsive desires.Your love and compassion (and prayers for them) may be the only Jesus they see.

LET OTHERS SEE JESUS IN YOU[3]

1) While passing through this world of sin, and others your life shall view,
Be clean and pure without, within, Let others see Jesus in you.(chorus)
Chorus: Let others see Jesus in you; Let others see Jesus in you;
Keep telling the story, be faithful and true,
Let others see Jesus in you.
2) Your life's a book before their eyes; They're reading it through and through;
Say, does it point them to the skies, Do others see Jesus in you? (chorus)
3) What joy 'twill be at set of sun, in mansions be-yond the blue,
To find some souls that you have won; Let others see Jesus in you. (chorus)

4) Then live for Christ both day and night, Be faithful, be
   brave, and true,
And lead the lost to life and light, Let others see Jesus in
   you. (Chorus)

**Titus 2:7 In everything set them an example by doing
what is good.**

**Ephesians 4:17 With the lord's authority let me say
this: live no longer as the ungodly do, for they are
hopelessly confused.**

**1ˢᵗ Tim 1:15,16 Here is a trustworthy saying
that deserves full acceptance: Christ Jesus came
into the world to save sinners—of whom I am
the worst. But for that very reason I was shown
mercy so that in me, the worst of sinners, Christ
Jesus might display His unlimited patience as an
example for those who would believe on Him and
receive eternal life.**

Paul reminds believers:

**In Ephesians 4:24-32 You must display a
new nature because you are a new person,
created in God's likeness--righteous, holy,
and true.**

**25) Therefore, putting away lying, "Let each
one of you speak truth with his neighbor,"
for we are members of one another.**

**26) "Be angry, and do not sin," do not let
the sun go down on your wrath,**

27) nor give place to the devil.

28) Let him who stole steal no longer, but rather let him labor, working with his hands what is good, that he may have something to give him who has need.

29) Let no corrupt word proceed out of your mouth, but what is good for necessary edification, that it may impart grace to the hearers,

30) And do not grieve the Holy Spirit of God, (our God) by whom you were sealed for the day of redemption.

31) Let all bitterness, wrath, anger, clamor, and evil speaking be put away from you, with all malice.

32) And be kind to one another, tender-hearted, forgiving one another, even as God in Christ forgave you.

FORGIVENESS

Isaiah 55:7 says it bluntly Let the wicked forsake (leave it behind) his way, and the unrighteous man his thoughts: Let him return to the Lord, and He will have mercy on him; And to our God, for He will abundantly pardon.(my parenthesis)

So many people today console themselves with, "Well, I'm not wicked...I'm a good person...but you love to get the "dirt" on your co-workers and tell others. Or..."I donate money to charity to help the poor"...but the housing you provide for them for government rent is poorly maintained and broken down. "I don't lie or steal...I visit my Mom or call once a week--mostly call."...but your Mom is lonely and feels forgotten. We are all guilty of something.

A selfish woman says, "It doesn't hurt to look lasciviously at that big hunk (a married man). I'm only flirting a little bit." He excuses his behavior by saying, "Well, she gave me that look."

There are many rationalizations for following up on our unrighteous thoughts...so we need to confess those unwholesome thoughts and ask God to forgive. These kinds of rationalized thinking are indulging in an unholy desire and may lead us into a relationship that will cause heartache for many.We need toPray for Him to help keep our thoughts pure and to turn away from any "worldly" temptations.

Isaiah wrote, HE WILL ABUNDANTLY PARDON...which is true; but, then stay away from those temptations and fill our minds with scripture...put on the armor of God--Read the WORD and Jesus will give us peace.

It is possible to turn our back on earthly pleasures-- difficult, but do-able with the help of the Holy Spirit. Many times a day, we can say, 'Lord, keep the "Deceiver" behind me (out of my mind) in the name of Jesus Christ"...that has been my weapon against the "minions of darkness" (Satan's puppets) since I became aware of our continuing spiritual battle against those "principalities of darkness," and myown sin-nature.

Therefore, if anyone is in Christ, he is a new creation; old things have passed away; behold, all things have become new. II Corinthians 5:17

Every time we find ourselves in our old behavior mode, our prayer should be to consciously try to get back to our "new" self which is in JESUS. Like me, you will likeyour "new" self so much better than your old "instant gratification of self" model.

And whenever you stand praying, if you have anything against anyone, forgive him, that your Father in heaven may also forgive you your trespasses. Mark 11:25

How true! If we have a hidden grudge against anyone, it can make us ill--mentally and spiritually. If we constantly search our minds to be sure we have truly forgiven friends, relatives, and even enemies whom we have felt slighted us in some way, God is a "JUST" God and will mete out forgiveness to us—IF we are willing to give it to others.

...Which I was not willing to do for my first husband for many years—unknowingly harboring that grudge *until a weekend visiting Heidi in Las Cruces only several weeks before Gerald passed away. Katrina had planned to visit her Father in Truth-or-Consequences on Sunday morning because the Veteran's Hospital had informed Heidi that Gerald was failing. Katrina felt she needed to reconcile her unforgiveness for her Father's broken promises throughout her growing up years. When she returned to Heidi's, we would eat lunch and then leave for Hobbs.*

The first time in my life I actually heard a "still small voice" was that Sunday morning when I was awakened at about 4:30 a.m. by the words "Go! Tell him about Jesus." When Katrina woke up, she was surprised when, ready so early, I told her I was going with her to see her Father.

Gerald said, "Yes! I want to accept Jesus as my personal Savior." And, "Yes! Would He please forgive my many sins."Praise the Lord, our God is a forgiving God.

Jesus knew when I obeyed his command that not only Gerald would now be at peace, but the burden of unforgiveness in my heart could be removed, as I was able to forgive not only Gerald, but also myself for my lack of trusting God in our marriage--and reacting to Gerald as the world would instead of how Jesus would(in our marriage.)Getting rid of that guilt relieved my heart and mind and opened both for Jesus to heal my soul.

Then Peter came to Jesus and asked, "Lord, how many times shall I forgive my brother when he sins against me? Up to seven times?" Jesus answered, "I tell you, not seven times, but seventy-seven times." Matthew 18:21

Blessings

But seek first His Kingdom and His righteousness, and all these things will be given to you as well. Matthew 6:33

When you are in His will, His blessings will pour out on you.

He watched over me, protected me, and loved me even when I was immersed in "self." Praise God, He was always with me...He never gave up on me, got me through trying times, gave me four healthy, loving children who are now loving adults, whom, I believe, are sold out to Jesus; that is not to say they are perfect. All four of them have gone from home and are going through their own trials and the same for my 15 grandchildren. My constant prayer is that they all believe the bible is the inerrant Word of God, and that they have a "quiet time" to read the Bible and follow God's directions.

How God has blessed me! I am forever amazed at how He has blessed me, even though I was such a "wayward" and "unseeing" child.

One neat thing Jesus said in **John 14:7 "if you had known Me, you would have known My Father also..."**

You know the Father by knowing the Son...and the Holy Spirit is helping you to learn to follow His will...could anything be easier? If we'll just eradicate our will (self-indulgence), trust in Him, and FOLLOW HIM. (Easier said than done, right?) Our old "sin-nature" is very difficult to eradicate (destroy), hence the warning...keep watch! For the "Deceiver" is forever close by, waitingfor that chink in the armor you have "put on" that day in your prayer and Bible Study. Pray unceasingly!

"It was then that Jonathan realized...realized that he had been going into an ambush and not only had the car been lifted over the danger areas but it had been transported some eighty miles down the road in less than a minute. Well, it had happened to the disciples in Galilee and to Phillip who was "caught away" from the Ethiopian Eunuch in Acts and certainly they were living in the Church Age or the Acts of the Holy Spirit. Our God is the same yesterday, today and forever. How the Spirit descended on the meeting that night as we celebrated. "We were caught up into His presence and continued in the power for almost four hours," Jonathan clearly remembers. What a victory! Once again, the devil had been defeated and the Lord had shown His mighty hand on the behalf of those who love Him. All the Lord requires is a yielded vessel, and, after all, his servant had become 'recklessly abandoned' for the Lord. 'It can happen to anyone,' explained Jonathan. 'All we have to do is be out there in that zone where the Spirit will move that way.' ...from RECKLESSLY ABANDONED, by Michael Howard."(My bold print)

TRUST HIM, uncompromisingly! Learn to never compromise with anything or anyone contrary to His Word. Then, with His help, we find the things of this world WILL "grow strangely dim."

To my brothers and sisters in Christ:

My brethren, count it all joy when you fall into various trials, knowing that the testing of your faith produces patience. But let patience have its perfect work, that you may be perfect and complete, lacking nothing. James 1:2-4

The trials we all go through might be terribly difficult, but believers are to consider them as opportunities for rejoicing. Troubles and difficulties are a tool the Lord uses to refine and purify our faith, producing patience and endurance

....that the genuineness of your faith, being much more precious than gold that perishes, though it is tested by fire, may be found to praise, honor, and glory at the revelation of Jesus Christ. 1st Peter 1:7

As the purity of gold is brought forth by intense heat, so the reality and purity of our faith are revealed as a result of the fiery trials we face. Ultimately, the testing of our faith not only demonstrates our final salvation, but also develops our capacity to bring glory to the Lord Jesus Christ here on earth and when He comes into His kingdom and we reign with Him.

...And not only that, but we also glory in tribulations, knowing that tribulation produces perseverance; and perseverance, character; and character, hope. Romans 5:3&4

Trials and tribulation produce endurance when we exercise faith during those difficult times. Such faith produces its own reward.

Blessed are those who are persecuted for righteousness'

sake, for theirs is the kingdom of heaven. Matthew 5:10

HALLELUJAH! That promise makes all the trials and tribulation worth the difficult times...when the Lord carries us...(because we trust Him)...when we stand in faith against the "onslaught" of the "Principalities of Darkness." (Satan and His minions)

He has shown you, O man, what is good; And what does the Lord require of you but to do justly, to love mercy, and to walk humbly with your God?Micah 6:8

He wants us to do justly... love mercy...walk humbly. These phrases summarize "biblical piety" in true worship. Sounds simple, but it is very difficult for us to exercise these standards consistently.

Do Justly...Who shows justice in everything we do? Most of the time "justice" to us is when we get what we want.

He guards the paths of justice, and preserves the way of His saints (us). Proverbs 2:8

Do we love mercy?... Maybe when it is convenient to our "life style." My thoughts now are coming from my own experience, and He is showing me how I "fooled" myself into thinking my way WAS being merciful. Most of the time, my mercy was available when I could squeeze it into my schedule and benefited me in some way.(such as, the donation could be taken off my income tax; or, they would send a free gift if I donated to their "worthy" cause.) Oftentimes, I questioned the charity's motives, when I should have been examining my heart to see if my "giving" was cheerful...not greedy for something "free".

So let each one give as he purposes in his heart, not grudgingly or of necessity; for God loves a cheerful giver. 2nd Corinthians9:7

"AND WHY DO YOU LOOK AT THE SPECK IN YOUR BROTHER'S EYE, BUT DO NOT CONSIDER THE PLANK IN YOUR OWN EYE... MATTHEW 7:3

Walk humbly with your God... My "walk" with the Lord is evidencing more humility every day; but, this last one is the most difficult to sustain because our old "self" keeps popping back into our mind and has to be banished by the Holy Spirit constantly. Thank you, Lord, for a RENEWAL of the "filling" of the Holy Spirit every time we ask for it...He is our only "restraining order" effective against the Principalities of Darkness who are waiting for the first sign of weakness in the wall the Holy Spirit maintains around our will power (against temptation.)

It is the Lord who ultimately gives us the strength, courage, and ability to exercise the "Virtues of Godly Living."

With much prayer and communication with our Lord, we will eventually understand how to practice these virtues in a Godly way instead of our way. Then, and only then, will we be able to live each day to its ultimate good in peace and joy and confidence about our eternal life.

Only then will we be "READY" for the New Jerusalem!

In Paul's letter to the Ephesian Church, he describes the blessings we possess:

The Blessings of Believers

(from[2b]NKJV STUDY BIBLE, second edition, 2007, published by /Thomas Nelson.)**(plus my** own comments)

I. We are chosen by God:

Ephesians 1:4) Just as He chose us in Him before the foundation of the world, that we should be holy and without blame before Him in love, 5) having predestined us to adoption as sons by Jesus Christ to Himself, according to the good pleasure of His will...

Even though I slept through (figuratively speaking) the first 46 years of my life, He didn't give up on me. He chose me early and knew I would eventually wake up to the fact that I need Him for sustenance...not only physically, but mentally--spiritually and emotionally (which are one and the same.) Every day before Satan is told to "get thee behind me in the name of Jesus Christ," I thank God profusely for choosing me and giving me the peace and joy of His Presence. And then I ask Him for a renewal of the filling of the Holy Spirit, because some of my thoughts and behaviors of the day before or the hour before or the minute before might have used up the power of the Holy Spirit, and it is necessary to start the day with the COMPLETE FILLING of Him in order to get through the day in His will.

II. We are adopted into God's family:

Ephesians 2:19 Now, therefore, you are no longer

strangers and foreigners, but fellow citizens with the saints and members of the household of God.

When you are truly filled with the Holy Spirit, it is very easy to love those family members of the saints, even one who might have constantly irritated you before you walked in God's will. This takes some time to develop, however, so don't be discouraged if you still have feelings of enmity now and then. Remember, there is only one perfect (sinless) man... And He is OUR SAVIOR--an example to strive to be like.

III. We are accepted before God.

Ephesians 1:6 to the praise of the glory of His grace, by which He made us accepted in the Beloved.

Jesus , the Son of God, made us acceptable to our Heavenly Father (Who cannot look on sin), by sacrificing Himself on the cross in order to take on our sins and cover them with His blood. Never could we imagine a love that great that one would give His life for us in order that we may spend eternity with Him! How can anyone deny that AWESOME LOVE?

IV. He forgives our sins.

Ephesians 1:7 In Him we have redemption through His blood, the forgiveness of sins, according to the riches of His grace...

We can be redeemed no matter how numerous and horrendous our sins are...thanks be to Jesus. Hope is restored in our despair because of His fulfilling sacrifice... He will help us repair and renew our lives from the minute we repent and accept that grace offered by God to all.

V. God gives us insight into His will.

Ephesians 1:8) which He made to abound toward us in all wisdom and prudence, 9) having made known to us the mystery of His will, according to His good pleasure which He purposed in Himself...

Especially if you are in the Word every day! And know His Voice in your prayers.

VI. We have an eternal inheritance.

Ephesians 1:11) In Him also we have obtained an inheritance, being predestined according to the purpose of Him who works all things according to the counsel of His will, 12) that we who first trusted in Christ should be to the praise of His glory.

This inheritance is the promise of eternal life in the company of our Savior and God...it is so satisfying to know where we will spend eternity...AND, to know no worry while we are still on this ol' earth, you can have that satisfaction, too, by walking in His Way.

VII. We are sealed by the Holy Spirit.

Ephesians 1:13) In Him you also trusted, after you heard the word of truth, the gospel of your salvation; in whom, also, having believed, you were sealed with the Holy Spirit of promise, 14) who is the guarantee of our inheritance until the redemption of the purchased possession, to the praise of His glory.

Being sealed with the Holy Spirit guarantees our salvation and our eternity with Christ...remember, though, that seal doesn't come unless you have a genuine, personal relationship with Him, communing with Him through your prayers, delving into the Word, and walking in love with Jesus and your fellow man. You can be filled with the Holy Spirit by believing: then, asking Jesus to fill you with the Holy Spirit. You will be surprised by the depth of emotion you will experience if you are truly sincere...it will "bowl you over."

VIII. We have God's mercy and love.

Ephesians 2:4,5. But God, Who is rich in mercy, because of His great love with which He loved us, 5) even when we were dead in trespasses (sins), made us alive together with Christ (by grace you have been saved).

Thank God for His rich mercy and love...and that He is like a patient parent who waited many, many years for me to acknowledge the fact that I cannot live without Him...and that He is now first in my life.

IX. He gives us wisdom and knowledge.

Ephesians 1:17) that the God of our Lord Jesus Christ, the Father of glory, may give to you the spirit of wisdom and revelation in the knowledge of Him, 18) the eyes of your understanding being enlightened; that you may know what is the hope of His calling, what are the riches of the glory of His inheritance in the saints.

HE IS SO GOOD! He gives us the wisdom to make the right decisions (if we ask) and, if we read the Word and use our ears to listen (Bible preaching), the knowledge of His Character to enhance our understanding of His glory... hence, AN INTIMATE RELATIONSHIP WITH OUR LORD, JESUS CHRIST! Thank you, Lord Jesus, for choosing me to receive this precious knowledge!

X. His Divine Power works in us.

Ephesians 1:19) and what is the exceeding greatness of His power toward us who believe, according to the working of His mighty power 20) which He worked in Christ when He raised Him from the dead and seated Him at His right hand in the heavenly places,

Ephesians 3:16) that He would grant you, according to the riches of His glory, to be strengthened with might (power) through His Spirit in the inner man, 17) that Christ may dwell in your hearts through faith; that you, being rooted and grounded in love, 18) may be able to comprehend, with all the saints what is the length and depth and height-- 19) to know the love of Christ which passes knowledge; that you may be filled with all the fullness of God. 20) Now to Him who is able to do exceedingly abundantly above all that we ask or think, according to the POWER that works in us

Can you imagine that we can tap a power source greater than anything in or on this world? There is a gospel song from a CD called, ULTIMATE POWER ANTHEMS OF THE CHRISTIAN FAITH, called "I Can Only Imagine…."which emphasizes the truth that we can only imagine what our life will be like with Jesus in the eternal Kingdom. It is impossible for us to even envision an iota of the incredible power of God; but, if we have the trust and faith in our hearts and minds, He can demonstrate that power in us. Hallelujah!

XI. Our spiritual being is given life!

Ephesians 2:1) And you He made alive, who were dead in trespasses and sins, 2) in which you once walked according to the course of this world, according to the

prince of the power of the air, the spirit who now works in the sons of disobedience, 3) among whom also we all once conducted ourselves in the lusts of our flesh, fulfilling the desires of the flesh and of the mind, and were by nature children of wrath, just as the others. 4) But God, who is rich in mercy, because of his great love with which He loved us, 5) even when we were dead in trespasses, made us alive together with Christ. (by grace you have been saved)

Thank you, Jesus!

XII. The promise of eternal kindness.

Ephesians 2:7 That in the ages to come He might show the exceeding riches of His grace in His kindness toward us in Christ Jesus.

Thank you for choosing me! Hallelujah! Amen!

XIII. The knowledge that God's plan for us is good.

Ephesians 2:10 For we are His workmanship, created in Christ Jesus for good works, which God prepared beforehand that we should walk in them.

It was hard to see this years ago, but with the "scales" off my eyes," He has shown me the truth--that He had plans for me from the time of my conception...even before then?

XIV. Unity and peace with all believers.

Ephesians 2:11) Therefore remember that you, once Gentiles in the flesh--who are called Uncircumcision by what is called the Circumcision made in the flesh by hands--12) that at that time you were without Christ,

being aliens from the commonwealth of Israel and strangers from the covenants of promise, having no hope and without God in the world. 13) But now in Christ Jesus you who once were "far off" have been brought near by the blood of Christ. 14) For He, Himself is our Peace, who Has made both one, and has broken down the middle wall of separation, 15) having abolished in His flesh the enmity, that of commandments contained in ordinances, so as to create in Himself one "new man" from the two, thus making peace, 16) and that He might reconcile them both to God in one body through the cross, thereby putting to death the enmity. 17) And He came and preached peace to you who were afar off and to those who were near. 18) For through Him we both have access by one Spirit to the Father.

Since He is making one "new man" by combining the one who is afar, (not only the Jews who were exiled from the Holy Land because they became "strangers from the covenants of promise," but also we who are grafted in to the family of Abraham, Isaac, and Jacob by the blood of Christ), with those brethren of Judah, who are still holding out for a Messiah who has not come yet...will realize that JESUS IS THEIR MESSIAH and that the Christians are truly one with them. Praise the Lord!

XV. Heavenly Citizenship

Ephesians 2:19 Now, therefore, you are no longer strangers and foreigners, but fellow citizens with the saints and members of the household of God

Praise be to God Who has made us one with His chosen people, and by finding our Jewish roots, we **are "PREPARED FOR THE NEW JERUSALEM"**

XVI. We have access to God through Christ.

Ephesians 3:11) according to the eternal purpose which He accomplished in Christ Jesus our Lord, 12) in Whom we have boldness and access with confidence through faith in Him.

Again I say, "Thank you, Jesus, from the bottom of my heart, where the Holy Spirit resides in me, that I can claim all of these blessings because You shattered the blinders I wore for so many years, not even realizing you have been preparing me for the New Jerusalem since the beginning of time!

"The God who thundered the Law from Mt. Sinai is the same God who stood on the hillside above the shores of Lake Galilee and expounded the deepest set of truths ever given to mankind. Without the Law, this set of truths could have no substance for they are solidly founded on the Ten Commandments and come out of them." (from the introduction of the book, SERMON ON THE MOUNT, by Michael Howard)

When these events happened, the groundwork was laid for the circling of time...until the time when the "far off" people of Israel (Jews and all true Christians) will be joined with the people of Israel (Jews from all over the world who have claimed Jesus as their Messiah) and the Judeans (Messianic Jews who never left Judea) .

Eventually, according to [1]**Colossians 3:10 And have put on the new man, which is renewed in knowledge after the image of him that created him.**

No one will remember sin and will simply bask in the light

and glory of Jesus' love. Until...all people of the Family of God will be restored to God's original "plan"...A NEW MAN, if you will...a "revuelto" (a turn-around) as the Spanish say...when trials are forgotten and will never be seen again...as the world would put it..."all sweetness and light".

However, this will not happen until the prophesies have been fulfilled; and, according to the book25 MESSIANIC SIGNS IN ISRAEL TODAY, by Noah W. Hutchings with Gilla Treibich, there are signs occurring in Israel that the Bible says will immediately precede the Great Tribulation and the coming of the Messiah.

To Christians, this means that Jesus Christ must be coming soon...for His Second coming.

To the Jew, this means a time of great persecution and trouble must come first (Some who study the Torah, --the books by Moses--think the Messiah is coming for the first time).

To the unbeliever, this means a time of slavish loyalty to the powers of darkness--the great "Deceiver"--you are not serving God and have not "professed Him before men," that means you are serving the Antithesis of God. (Satan) Sorry to have to repeat this...but, that's the way it is.

If you don't have a personal relationship with Jesus, you are not only missing the peace and joy He gives you; but you're missing out on eternal life with Him. Think about your future...you need to get on God's side!

JESUS IS THE RIGHT SIDE! AGAIN...LORD GOD, OUR GOD... THANK YOU!

THE GARDEN TOMB

Even though it was not cold that last day of the tour, when I saw the opening which led into the garden tomb, where Joseph of Arimathea laid the linen-wrapped body of Jesus, shivers ran up and down my spine. Here was where Jesus was buried after he died on the cross FOR ME AND FOR YOU! And He was walking in this very garden after His resurrection. The myriad of emotions coursing through my body and mind was a new experience for me and was a powerful precursor to the communion we took in a small chapel up a slight incline from the tomb.

There is a song which pops into my consciousness quite often these days...started about six months ago and is so fitting at times in our walk with Jesus:

[4]TURN YOUR EYES UPON JESUS...LOOK FULL IN HIS WONDERFUL FACE,

AND THE THINGS OF EARTH WILL GO STRANGELY DIM... IN THE LIGHT OF HIS GLORY AND GRACE.

Standing by the Garden Tomb that day, I wanted to belt out that chorus in the worst way because of His victory over death and Satan...and His sacrifice that "saved a wretch like me." How can anyone not choose JESUS and LIFE?

Isaiah 45:22 Look unto Me, and be ye saved, all the ends of the earth.

Read the words of this song and think how deeply Helen Lemmuel must have felt toward her Savior and Friend:
1.) [4]O soul, are you weary and troubled? No Light in the darkness you see?

There's Light for a look at the Savior,And life more abundant and free!

2.) Through death into Life everlasting, He passed, and we follow Him there,

Over us sin no more hath dominion--For more than con-qu'rors we are

3.) His Word will not fail you, He promised; Believe Him and all will be well;

Then go to a world that is dying, His perfect salvation to tell!

The chorus of the song (in caps above) is enough for you to memorize and sing whenever you might be angry, frustrated, impatient with a situation and maybe out of control...sing it in your mind or even out loud; and surprisingly, you will feel a calmness and a peace that will help you solve the problem, whatever the trial is at that particular time. When I was being attacked by Satan's minions, to remind myself to turn my eyes upon Jesus was enough to lock the Deceiver out. AND, it will remind you to make decisions that will give our Lord the glory, and he will pour more grace down on you. Blessings will flow and the Light will stream out of you onto the ones around you. Believe me, He is there and waiting for you to give Him that glory.

The chorus of the hymn says...⁴LOOK FULL IN HIS WONDERFUL FACE." The neat thing is...His face comes into our sight when we pray fervently and squeeze our eyes shut at the same time and zero in on the light that fuses behind our eyelids in the shape of His face. One might say, "It's all in your imagination." I choose to believe I have LOOKED FULL IN HIS WONDERFUL FACE because it is true...the things of this world grow strangely dimmer and dimmer in importance in our daily living. If we stay in His will, during early morning prayers, Jesus will wrap us in His arms and assure us He will be with us all day with a "hedge of protection" in an aura of His Light round about us. SWEET!

SPEAKING OF SACRIFICE...

The Lord, Our Lord, is blessed when we follow His will and when our actions give glory to His name. (And, on the other hand, imagine how wounded He feels when we fail Him and give in to our sin-nature doing even little things that we know would disappoint Him.) Remember... He sacrificed His Son for us.

If we are truly sold out to Jesus, we are devastated when He is disappointed in us...and feel that we need to sacrifice ourselves anew, and be cleansed from our repugnant behavior for His sake.

It is difficult to believe that when Solomon finished (following God's directions to the letter) and dedicated the Temple of God, he sacrificed 22,000 bulls and 120,000 sheep for the dedication ceremony.

2nd Chronicles 7:8) At that time, Solomon kept the feast seven days, and all Israel with him, a very great assembly from the entrance of Hamath to the Brook of Egypt, 9) And on the eighth day they held a sacred assembly, for they observed the dedication of the altar seven days and the feast seven days. They did this simply to glorify God!

True, they were set up for Holy Sacrifices in those days of the First Covenant; however, how long has it been since you have even sacrificed several hours of your time in God's service or even an hour on Wednesday evening for Bible study with your soul mates...the Family of God? How long has it been since you have been on fire for Jesus and showed that enthusiasm to those around you?

How long has it been that we have had thousands of people come together to worship our Lord and Savior?(as one voice). Maybe the tea parties could be set on fire for God; and we could win over (with our faith) anyone who tries to advocate our adversary, Satan, from within. All we have to do is pray as one voice.

A good verse to memorize…2nd **Chronicles 7:14 says…"If my people, who are called by my name, will humble themselves, pray, seek my face, and turn from their wicked ways, I will hear from heaven, forgive them of their sins, and heal their land."**

He will hear genuine repentance and honor it. He will know if we are sincere and truly want the glory for Him and not ourselves. He will save our country and help us to make it great again…if that is His will and IF we are truly sorry, as a nation.

Whatever His will, HIS FAITHFULNESS IS GREAT:

[9]GREAT IS THY FAITHFULNESS

Great is Thy faithfulness, O God my Father.
There is no shadow of turning with Thee;
Thou changest not, Thy compassions they fail not;
as Thou hast been, Thou forever wilt be.

Summer and winter, and spring-time and harvest,
Sun, moon, and stars in their courses above…
Join with all nature in man-i-fold witness…
To thy great faithfulness, mercy and love.

Pardon for sin and a peace that endureth,
Thy own dear Presence to cheer and to guide...
Strength for today and bright hope for tomorrow,
Blessings all mine, with ten thousand beside!

Great is Thy faithfulness! Great is Thy faithfulness!
Morning by morning new mercies I see;
All I have needed Thy Hand hath provided...
Great is Thy faithfulness, Lord, unto me.

A hymn for encouragement, love, and remembrance of His mercy...

How could anyone turn from Jesus or not let Him in their life after singing and meditating on this song? Perhaps some have never heard this song. Perhaps some do not have "ears" to hear the message even when they are told about Jesus.

How can anyone choose death over life everlasting? How could anyone decide for the evil one who only wants to destroy them? Perhaps some haven't realized that pleasing "self" at any cost could mean the loss of their soul. **Help us, O Lord, to reach those lost souls.**

ONLY GOD, OUR GOD, can soften a heart enough to change a "mindset" to acknowledge His Lordship in their life. All we can do is pray and be "available" to join where He is working and do His will.

Remember what Jesus said in Revelation 3:15-21 "I know thy works, that thou art neither cold nor hot; I would thou wert cold or hot, So then because thou art lukewarm, and neither cold nor hot, I will spew (vomit) thee out of my mouth."

Let's wake up and pull our toe out of the "world". Instead of lukewarm, let's be "on fire" for Him who created us and blesses us and loves us more than we know and more than we are willing to admit. Let's shed our "old self" so a shiny, clean new being can dedicate the rest of our lives to our Savior and Creator and Lord. We will never be perfect, but with Him, we can be free.

Because you say, 'I am rich, have become wealthy, and have need of nothing'--and do not know that you are wretched, miserable, poor, blind, and naked--I counsel you to buy from Me gold refined in the fire, that you may be rich; and white garments that you may be clothed, that the shame of your nakedness may not be revealed; and anoint your eyes with eye salve, that you may see.

Money is just a thing...not important ...JESUS IS YOUR PROTECTOR AND YOUR PROVIDER...He is EVERLASTING LIFE AND HE'S COMING BACK TO TAKE HIS PEOPLE. WILL YOU BE ONE OF THEM?

As many as I love, I rebuke and chasten. Therefore, be zealous and repent.

Behold, I stand at the door and knock. If anyone hears My voice and opens the door, I will come in to him and dine with him, and he with Me.

To him who overcomes, I will grant to sit with me on my throne, as I also overcame and sat down with my Father on His throne." Rev.3:15-21

A Note to Jesus:

You are such a good friend to have because you never leave me, and are always "on call"...even if I forget you when I get distracted doing "things" not connected with my "commitment to You." You are leading me to the place where those "things" no longer matter...where I can hear Your voice even though You don't even say anything.

One thing...being sold out to You is sure good for the sinuses, 'cause I cry a lot, which gets the juices flowing. When I was in Western Ill University, someone told me it was good for your health to have a good cry at least once a week...You keep me crying every morning when You wake me up with Your words to add to this book. I hope those whom You are nudging, (actually imploring, in these latter days) to wake up from their slumber (and stop being lukewarm because you will not know them) and realize You want them to be "sold out to YOU" ...not only in words...but so completely that every cell in their body is involved in You. Purify their cells, take out negative foreign matter (Satan) and make them well, physically, morally, and SPIRITUALLY...which should be in another order...SPIRITUALLY, morally, and physically. Thank you, Jesus, for choosing me to choose You, because my life is yours...and in giving it to You, I CHOSE LIFE ETERNAL. Sincerely, Your child of God...Sister Carol

Giving my Whole Self to Jesus

It is hard for me to fathom this, because I have been brought up in my family and in society to care for number one...myself...so it is almost impossible to relinquish my cells to ANYONE even after physical death (donating organs to science) because one tends to be possessive of "self" even though it no longer matters; however, when one realizes it does matter "humongously" (a word my granddaughter, Grace, taught me and fits perfectly). Our eternal life depends upon turning those cells over to The Lord, Jesus (not letting Satan use them when he can entice you to forget about your covenant with Jesus and you take a little step back into the world for just a moment.)

We have not quite made it to the point where we can say the devil can't touch us because we have been bought and paid for and we are completely sold out to Jesus. Until we remember to pray every morning and every minute for Jesus to permeate our every cell so there is no room for Satan to get a foothold, (with just a little germ to make our body sick or just a little negative thought to nourish that "germ"), we cannot keep him out. He is very pervasive and can deceive so easily if we don't have our guard (Jesus) up.

One very effective way the "Deceiver" can accomplish his evil plans is to figure out our weaknesses, keep chipping away by little insidious reminders of our sin(s) which God has already forgiven, and then full scale attack with devastating guilt thoughts, which might turn into "just one more time." **Run from those thoughts!**Turn to prayer and scripture.

I find that if my prayers were simply perfunctory (done as a matter of duty) that morning and/or I didn't request fervently, "Satan, get thee behind me in the name of Jesus," I have left my mind unprotected from his invasion (Satan's demons attack full scale, when we become sold out to the Lord). My sojourn in this world has been too long as a lost person (who didn't even know it); thereby making it more difficult for me to remember that if I am in the will of God and putting Him first as I should be, that Satan's barbs cannot pierce God's armor.

Tight Rein on our Mouth

I should have put on that armor by reading my Bible and praying diligently...OR sought God's will about decisions instead of letting my mouth run ahead of my prayers. There is a Bible verse that indicates we need to keep a tight rein on our mouth...

Ephesians 4:29) Let no corrupt word proceed out of your mouth, but what is good for necessary edification, that it may impart grace to the hearers, 30) and do not grieve the Holy Spirit of God, by whom you were sealed for the day of redemption.

When I look back over the years, the times I have "put my foot in my mouth" still haunt me; so, it is really not a good idea to reminisce about your past unless you are evaluating your "walk" with Jesus or considering a safe topic which is an uplifting subject (not reminiscing about how bad you were or the "sly old Fox" might tempt you away from concentrating on Jesus...the "Deceiver" is very good at that).

Maybe you have already come to the point of where people wonder if you are nuts 'cause it looks like you are talking to yourself when actually you are either praising God in thanks or just asking advice from the Holy Spirit with your lips moving or actually speaking out loud. I have come to that point and I thank Him every day for choosing me. (sometimes every second) I'm getting closer--Praise God!

The Lordship of Christ

"True salvation produces a heart that voluntarily responds to the ever-awakening reality of Christ's lordship." From [6]THE GOSPEL ACCORDING TO JESUS, by John MacArthur, Jr. 1988, 1993, 2008, Zondervan.

More and more I am learning about My Lord Jesus Christ... and He is my LORD--I am HIS SLAVE and His bond servant. I not only want to serve Him with humility...I am obligated to obey Him to the fullest. If my purpose for using my God-given abilities is to glorify Him, then He is truly my Lord. If my purpose is to gain praise for myself, then I will be the last when His Kingdom comes...but, if my aim is to glorify Jesus, then I will be among the first in His glorious Kingdom on earth. Neat promise, hey what?

[6]John Macarthur in THE GOSPEL ACCORDING TO JESUS, says, "No one can be saved who is either <u>unwilling to obey Christ or consciously, callously rebellious against His lordship.</u>"

Matthew 19:30 But many who are first will be last, and the last first.

It has taken me long to recognize that Jesus not only became my Savior when I was "born again," but he also became My LORD.

Ephesians 5: 17) Therefore do not be unwise, but understand what the will of the Lord is

18) And do not be drunk with wine, in which is dissipation; but be filled with the Spirit,

19) speaking to one another in Psalms and hymns and spiritual songs, singing and making melody in your heart to the Lord,

20) giving thanks always for all things to God the Father in the name of our Lord Jesus Christ,

21) submitting to one another in the fear (respect) of God.

The people of Noah's time scoffed at Noah because they thought they could behave in outrageous ways and not obey the commands of God...and there would be no consequences (as they had been doing whatever they wanted for so long and there had been no "punishment").

That whole story is so similar to what is going on today. God is slow to anger, but He eventually gets fed up. Praise God He chose you and me to drop the scales from our eyes, so we can be living for Him by taking his instructions from His WORD, and we will be ready for His return at all times. The oil for our lamps is stored in a safe and convenient place...in our hearts with the Holy Spirit.

Joy

The joy I feel every day and all day long suffuses through my body regularly to remind me I am His and available for His command. When I remember to claim His power, He sends it to me full measure and I feel so blessed I just want everyone to have what He has given me... Peace and Joy!!!! No time in the past have I ever felt this completeness, because HE IS WHAT MAKES ME COMPLETE! If you haven't felt this completeness yet... pray, read your Bible, talk with others in our family of God...it will come!

A slave to my Lord...yes, and I praise Him every day in every way until He comes again in person!

Listen to the joy my friend, Jennifer, has after several years of consistent, sincere prayer to our Lord: Jennifer was beginning to wonder if she would ever find a man who would meet her very necessary qualifications. She was thirty and she so wanted to have a child before her time clock ran out. We began praying—one year, two years—three years went by. Today, she not only has a wonderful Christian husband, but God has blessed her with Brooke, a teen-aged daughter and two babies-- twins, a boy and a girl. Isn't God good!

Perseverance in your faith, perseverance in your prayer, perseverance in your obedience will bring joy immeasurable, and eternal life with Him.

I praise God for His patience and steadfast love and forever thank Him for choosing me to be the recipient of both for eternity.

In his letter to the Ephesians, Paul lists **the Responsibilities of the Followers of Christ**[2b]**...**

I. To keep the unity of the Spirit...

Ephesians 4:1) I (Paul), therefore, the prisoner of the Lord, beseech you to walk worthy of the calling with which you were called, 2) with all lowliness and gentleness,

with longsuffering,, bearing with one another in love, 3) endeavoring to keep the unity of the Spirit in the bond of peace. 4) There is one body and one Spirit, just as you were called in one hope of your calling; 5) one Lord, one faith, one baptism; 6) one God and Father of all, Who is above all, and through all, and in you all.

It is possible for the body of believers to keep the unity of the Spirit if we remember to put Him first in everything...to pray about everything, singly and corporately,...and to all be of one mind in Christ...especially to pray for each other to "KEEP THE FAITH" and for good health, and to love and support each other in God's peace.

II. To use our abilities for the church's benefit...

Ephesians 4:7) But to each one of us grace was given according to the measure of Christ's gift. 8) Therefore He says: "When He ascended on high, He led captivity captive, and gave gifts to men."

11) And He Himself gave some to be apostles, some prophets, some evangelists, and some pastors and teachers, 12) for the equipping of the saints for the work of ministry, for the edifying of the body of Christ,

13) till we all come to the unity of the faith, and the knowledge of the Son of God, to a perfect man, to the measure of the stature of the fullness of Christ;

He bestowed the gift of compassion and empathy upon me at *a very young age; however, when my singing voice became mature at about age 16, the praise of people became more important to me than using that gift (singing duets and praising the Lord with my best friend, Mary Hurt, at her church on Sundays). Gratifying my teen-age desires of fame, career, and wealth became uppermost in my mind...a habitual way of thinking that actually pushed God's way of thinking way to the back of my consciousness (except when I heard a sermon which went directly to my stored-away data and nudged at my heart.) But, being so immersed in self, I would rationalize by saying, "A loving God would want the best for me as I'm going through these teen-age years." (My problem was...I really didn't know what was best for me in those early yearsand even now); and, if I had listened to Jesus then, I might have used the gifts He had given me sooner for His Kingdom of Believers; however, as I said before, He knew my story from way back when, and it played out exactly as he has written it...and exactly as He is telling me to write it now, perhaps or probably BECAUSE He will use my story to wake up someone like He used Jack and more than a few friends to get me back on that narrowpath to Jesus.*

III. WE NEED TO KEEP GROWING AND MATURING.

Ephesians 4:14) that we should no longer be children, tossed to and fro and be carried about with every wind of doctrine (differentdenominations), by the trickery of men, in the cunning craftiness of deceitful plotting, 15) but speaking the truth in love, may grow up in all things into Him Who is the head--Christ—(my parenthesis)

In all of my wanderings to and fro, Jesus was with me always and kept me from wandering so far that I couldn't get back to THE WAY...which, of course, is HIM. When I think about how far I explored "outer space" (which is where you are if you are not walking with Him), my mind is blown away to realize He does not give up on anybody... they can be restored if they sincerely repent and open their heart and mind to Him!

IV. IT IS NECESSARY TO PUT AWAY OLD, SINFUL WAYS..

Ephesians 4:17) This I say, therefore, and testify in the Lord, that you should no longer walk as the rest of the Gentiles walk, in the futility of their mind, 18) having their understanding darkened, being alienated from the life of God, because of the ignorance that is in them, because of the blindness of their heart; 19) who, being past feeling, have given themselves over to lewdness, to work all uncleanness with greediness. 20) But you have not so learned Christ,21) if indeed you have heard Him and have been taught by Him, as the truth is in Jesus: 22) that you put off , concerning your former conduct, the old man which grows corrupt according to the deceitful lusts, 23) and be renewed in the spirit of your mind,24) and that you put on the new man which was created according to God, in true righteousness and holiness.

We are a new "man" since the Holy Spirit infused our being...meaning we put our focus on the things of God; and use the authority He gives us over the "Deceiver" to say "No!" to former desires.

V. We are to speak honestly and purely.

Ephesians 4:24) And that you put on the new man which was created according to God, in true righteousness and holiness. 29) Let no corrupt word proceed out of your mouth, but what is good for necessary edification, that it may impart grace to the hearers...

It took me many years after I was saved to "put on the new man" completely; of course, the old Carol tries to rear up every once in a while...but, you know what? God's mercy and goodness is steadily "sanctifying" (purifying my thoughts and actions) so even though our adversary

(Satan and his minions) keeps trying new ways to wiggle into my thoughts, tries to get me to join "pity parties," and insidiously attempts to send me on "guilt trips" (mostly to distract my thoughts away from the peace Jesus has guaranteed me), I have learned to "put on the armor of God" every morning by studying His Word, praying, (not necessarily in that order) and staying still to hear His Voice.

VI. We are to do what the Spirit leads us to do.

Ephesians 4:30 And do not grieve the Holy Spirit of God, by whom you were sealed for the day of redemption.

PRAISE THE LORD...how can I grieve Him...HE WHO HAS GIVEN ME SO MUCH! My very life...my very soul...my very existence!!! For ETERNITY! He has given me the ability to love others; when before I only wanted self-gratification. He has given me unparalleled love; when before I thought I was "unlovable;" He has given me security beyond measure; when before I thought I had to "earn" providence, because no one else would be there for me; He has given me a "peace that passeth all understanding!" HALLELUJAH!

VII. We need to imitate God.

Ephesians 5:1 Therefore be imitators of God as dear children.

My late-blooming understanding is--the reason we need to learn more and more about our God, our Savior, our Holy Spirit is so we can be more and more like Him every day in every way. He gives us eyes to see, ears to hear, and a mind to focus on HIM. Children are wonderful imitators... it is the duty of the parents to nurture a knowledge of and a desire to be like the Heavenly Father(by the parents' example of a loving faith in JesusChrist). Also, remember the Adversary is very good at what he does--the "CEO" of "Distractions, Inc." There are so many habits, like reading romantic novels, watching thrilling movies, working to earn a "living," that keep us from thinking about our spiritual health (Jesus).My thoughts are, "Why didn't I come to this realization before now?" He only gives us what we can handle--negative trials or positive blessings--it works.

VII. Our purpose is to walk in love.

Ephesians 5:2 And walk in love, as Christ also has loved us and given Himself for us, an offering and a sacrifice to God for a sweet smelling aroma.

When we ask ourselves while making a decision, WHAT WOULD JESUS DO? We are sending a sweet-smelling aroma up to Him when we follow a decision made on that basis (of love)...IF we have been in the WORD and know enough about our Lord to know how he would react to a situation such as the one we have, it will be the right decision. So, our sacrifice on God's altar is our time, in that case, to have a closer relationship with our Savior so we know Him as well as ourselves (and don't let the adversary in to voice an opinion) **That takes prayer and lots of it!**

IX. Study the Word to find out what is acceptable to the Lord.

Ephesians 5:8) Ephesians 5:8-10 For you were once darkness, but now you are light in the Lord. Walk as children of light for the fruit of the Spirit is in all goodness, righteousness, and truth, finding out what is acceptable to the Lord.

The more we read His Word, the more we wake up to what we HAVEN'T been doing. Such as...turning off the TV (even the news) when it begins showing stories about very bad people doing very bad things. Or...stopping corruptible talk or leave before it gets into our mind and affects our thinking...such as gossip, an off-color joke, or someone using unacceptable language...or someone actually deliberately talking against our Lord. It is necessary to be with other children of God for support and knowledge of God's will, to read the Bible regularly, and go to Sunday School and worship service to "hear" what is acceptable to Him. The closer we get in our personal relationship with Him, He will talk with us andwe feel His loving acceptance of our behavior; or, perhaps silence and consequences if not acceptable.

X. He adjures us to make the most of our time.

Ephesians 5:15) See then that you walk circumspectly, not as fools but as wise, 16) redeeming the time, because the days are evil.

Our time should be spent wisely as we have but a short time to "tell" more people about Jesus. If we are fulfilling our purpose in God's Kingdom (go and tell) and, trying to wake up the "slumbering Christian" by reminding them of what's coming according to the scriptures; then, we are definitely using our time wisely.

Some Christians are resting on their "laurels," however. Because they feel they are "ready" for the New Jerusalem simply because they are saved and know they will not lose that salvation, many will not be diligent in telling others about Jesus and eternal life. An alert Christian, though, surely is feeling an urgency to do more to get the WORD to others, and is using their time to witness and "tell" every person Godsends us.

XI. He will fill us with the Spirit every time we ask.

Ephesians 5:18 And do not be drunk with wine, in which is dissipation, but be filled with the Spirit...

It is not difficult to understand God's will, if we are filled with His Spirit; however, reading the Bible and praying much is an inspiration to want to be filled anew every day...so the Adversary can't sneak in and build a barrier to inhibit your desire for the Holy Spirit to infill you completely. He has a cunning that is beyond our comprehension; so, we need that infusion of the Holy Spirit every day IN JESUS NAME.

XII. We need to submit to one another.

Ephesians 5:21 SUBMITTING TO ONE ANOTHER IN THE FEAR OF GOD.

SUBMITTING does not necessarily mean being under the absolute control of another; but more like voluntarily placing oneself under the authority of another, or showing the love of Christ by serving.

We have a lady in our church, Sister Barbara, who takes joy in cooking and serving others, giving of her time and resources for her brothers and sisters in Christ, and ministering to those who are lost.

XIII. To have marriages that honor God.

Ephesians 5:33 Nevertheless, Let each one of you in particular so love his own wife as himself, and let the wife see that she respects her husband.

Carol L. Briggs

Just as Christ is not inferior to the Father, but is the second person in the Trinity, wives are equal to their husbands, yet in the marriage relationship, a husband and wife have different roles. A wife's voluntary submission arises out of her own submission to Christ.

Love and joy to you and peace be with you from God our Father and the Lord Jesus Christ.

"As the Father loved me, I also have loved you; abide in my love. If you keep my commandments, you will abide in My love, just as I have kept My Father's commandments and abide in His love. These things I have spoken to you, that my joy may remain in you, and that your joy may be full." John 15:9-11

We sometimes forget the joy we have because He chose us...if we keep our thinking on Him, the joy should be bubbling from our countenance constantly so others can see how abiding in His love can fill us with joy and love for each other. Our "FAITH" brings us not only love and joy...but security in His love. (PEACE) Love, joy, and peace comes from trusting Him! A song to sing:

HAVE FAITH IN GOD[3]

1st verse...Have faith in God when your pathway is lonely,
He sees and knows all the way you have trod;
Never alone are the least of His children;
have faith in God, have faith in God. (C)
CHORUS: HAVE FAITH IN GOD, HE'S ON HIS THRONE;
HAVE FAITH IN GOD, HE WATCHES O'ER HIS OWN;

HE CANNOT FAIL, HE MUST PREVAIL; HAVE FAITH IN GOD,
HAVE FAITH IN GOD.
2nd...Have faith in God when your pray'rs are unanswered, your earnest plea...He will never forget;
Wait on the Lord, trust His Word and be patient, Have faith in God, He'll answer yet. (C)
3rd...Have faith in God in your pain and your sorrow, His heart is touched with your grief and despair,
Cast all your cares and your burdens upon Him, And leave them there, oh, leave them there.(C)
4th...Have faith in God tho' all else fail a-bout you; Have faith in God, He provides for His own;
He cannot fail tho' all kingdoms shall perish, He rules, He reigns up-on His throne. (C)

No one can sing this song without being reminded of His promises all throughout the Bible...unless the one singing completely disregards the words and doesn't think about them at all. (this is what I did for many years...although many of those years, I didn't sing hymns at all.)

As soon as the Lord shed those scales from my eyes, (when I finally realized that He is the Lord of my life, not me) I not only began to understand every scripture I read and was able to incorporate it into my life, but, every hymn or chorus I sang or heard began to touch me much more deeply than ever before...mind and heart were affected as well as emotions which opened my tear ducts profusely and frequently. He not only healed my painful feet malady, He poured the Holy Spirit over and into me so fully that the hardcore developed from childhood was melted and my new birth resulted in an ability to love others I had never felt before.

All I can keep saying is, "Thank you, Jesus, for choosing me!" And, He did choose me...

(Ephesians 1:4) He chose us in Him before the foundation of the world, that we should be holy and without blame before Him in love, 5) having predestined us to adoption as sons by Jesus Christ to himself, according to the good pleasure of His will, 6) to the praise of the glory of His grace, by which He made us accepted in the Beloved.

In Romans 5:1) therefore, having been justified by FAITH, we have peace with God through our Lord Jesus Christ, 2) through whom we also have access by FAITH into this grace in which we stand, and rejoice in hope of the glory of God.

Christian Definition of FAITH: We cannot see the outcome; we are not sure what lies ahead (Heb. 11:1), but we are convinced of the REALITY OF GOD (Heb. 11:6). (dictionary definition--Belief or trust in someone or something without logical proof) (The Bible is our proof)

Mark 11: 22-24 So Jesus answered and said to them, "Have faith in God. For assuredly, I say to you, whoever says to this mountain. 'Be removed and be cast into the sea,' and does not doubt in his heart, but believes that those things he says will be done, he will have whatever he says. Therefore I say to you, whatever things you ask when you pray, believe that you receive them, and you will have them."

ABOUT THE "NEW JERUSALEM...

Revelations 21:5 Then He who sat on the throne said, "Behold, I make all things new." And He said to me, "Write, for these words are true and faithful."

The believers' rebirth through faith in Christ brings newness to that person's life, but it is only in the eternal state that God will "make all things new." (paraphrase from,[2b] NKJV STUDY BIBLE)

NEW JERUSALEM (Greek--Hierousalem kaine) The Greek term denotes ""the brand new Jerusalem."

The New Jerusalem that comes out of heaven is plainly distinct from the earthly Jerusalem, the former capital of Israel. This is the city Abraham looked for, the city that has foundations, whose builder and maker is God. (1) This is the city that exists even now in heaven, for Paul calls it the Jerusalem that is above.(2)

(1) Hebrews 11:8-10 By faith Abraham obeyed when he was called to go out to the place which he would receive as an inheritance. And he went out, not knowing where he was going. By faith he dwelt in the land of promise as in a foreign country, dwelling in tents with Isaac and Jacob, the heirs with him of the same promise; for he waited for the city which has foundations, whose builder and maker is GOD.

(2) Galatians 4:26 but the Jerusalem above is free, which is the mother of us all.

Just as the apostle John saw the New Jerusalem descending from heaven (Rev.21), so Ezekiel envisioned the day when the city of God would finally be made perfect and complete in every way. Both prophets saw twelve gates facing the four corners of the earth (Ezek. 48:31-34; Rev. 21:12, 13), an indication of accessibility for everyone inscribed with the names of the twelve tribes of Israel.

The gates suggest inclusion, restoration, and fulfillment of all that God has promised His covenant people. In John's vision, this image is strengthened by the fact that these gates never shut. (paraphrasing Rev. 21:25).

This is a strong hope we can look forward to with great anticipation. Right now, we may sometimes feel distant from God, perhaps alone and confused and wondering whether he even knows who we are. The assurance of scripture is that someday we will no longer wonder where God is, we will be with HIM--forever!

Revelation 3:12 He who overcomes, I will make him a pillar in the temple of my God, and he shall go out no more. I will write on him the name of My God, and the name of the city of My God, the New Jerusalem, which comes down out of heaven from my God. And I will write on Him My new name.

"He who has an ear, let him hear what the Spirit says to the churches." Rev. 3:13

Can you hear it? **We will be the pillars in the temple of God.** The key words in that verse are

"HE WHO OVERCOMES!" Overcomes what?...the "wiles"(temptations) of anything other than Jesus.

My conclusion is...while we are living in today's world, we can turn our backs on 'THE THINGS OF THIS WORLD" by staying in the LIGHT OF HIS GLORY AND GRACE...and live in and with that Light until He comes for us to reside with HIM in THE NEW JERUSALEM in love and peace FOREVER! Wow!

Are you allowing Him to prepare you for the New Jerusalem?

Think about it!

SEEK THE LORD WHILE HE MAY BE FOUND, CALL UPON HIM WHILE HE IS NEAR.

LET THE WICKED FORSAKE HIS WAY, AND THE UNRIGHTEOUS MAN HIS THOUGHTS;

LET HIM RETURN TO THE LORD, AND HE WILL HAVE MERCY ON HIM; FOR HE WILL ABUNDANTLY PARDON ISAIAH 55:6.7

But those who wait on the Lord shall renew their strength; They shall mount up with wings like eagles, they shall run and not be weary, They shall walk and not faint. Isaiah 40:31

Let Him Return to the Lord

On March 3, 2009, when Jack slipped down to the floor and it was impossible for me to raise his inert form back up to his feet, he was 91 years old; he had had six more years of a peaceful life after his first stroke in 2003. The ER people came, checked his vitals, and lifted him onto the stretcher...he seemed to be all right; but, after 20 days in the TC wing, eight days in the Hobbs Health care unit, and six days at home, Jack went to be with Jesus...

On April 5th, Katrina, my youngest daughter, had told Ursula that she and her girls had visited Grandpa after church and that he recognized Grace, his littlest Granddaughter, who was his best friend, (besides Jesus)... but that he seemed to be somewhat disoriented and was probably going to be leaving us soon; that if Roxanne and Hannah, Ursula's daughters, wanted to see their Grandpa once more before he left, go see him that afternoon—and they did. He opened his eyes when Hannah talked to him, but they didn't stay open. I think he heard their voices and knew they were there for him.

At 4:30 a.m. on April 6, I woke up to a restless rustling noise coming from Jack's bed. My first thought was to rub his forehead and wash his face. He had indicated that he knew the girls the day before when they visited him; but, now he didn't even open his eyes to smile at me. So, after I had tucked the pillow behind Jack and made him comfortable, I put on the music of Anne Murray; she was singing, "I am climbing Jacob's Ladder." Whilesmoothing his forehead and telling him, "I love you," it became apparent he had gone up that ladder into the arms of Jesus. My praises were to God who had given Jack a healthy, fruitful life and a pain-free, peaceful death. His purpose in God's plan had been fulfilled, and God took him home.

When our dying bodies have been transformed into bodies that will never die, this Scripture will be fulfilled: **"Death is swallowed up in victory. O death, where is your victory? O death, where is your sting? For sin is the sting that results in death, and the law gives sin its power. But thank God! He gives us victory over sin and death through our Lord, Jesus Christ. 1 Corinthians 15:54-57**

Hebrews 6:10 God is not unjust. He will not forget how hard you have worked for Him and how you have shown your love to Him by caring for other believers, as you still do.

This book is my purpose...to help remind believers to be out there "telling" others that God's love is sufficient for all.

When you obey my commandments, you remain in my love, just as I obey my Father's commandments and remain in His love. I have told you these things so that you will be filled with my joy. Yes, your joy will overflow! John 15:10-11

...AND MINE HAS!

Bibliography and Footnote referrals

1. RECKLESSLY ABANDONED, BY Michael Howard,1996, 3rd Edition, 200l, Out of Africa Publishing, Kansas City, MO.

2. Scriptural references:

   a) Scripture taken from THE HOLY BIBLE, NIV Version, 1973, 1978, 1984, International BibleSociety. Used by permission.

   b) NKJSB, 2nd Edition, 1997, 2007, Thomas Nelson Publishing. Used by permission.

3. The words of the hymns taken from: THE BAPTIST HYMNAL, 1991, Convention Press.

4. Used by permission given from individual copyright for each hymn or song.

5. The words of the hymns taken from: HYMNS OF FAITH, 1980, Tabernacle Publishing Co. (A Division of Hope Publishing Company.) Used by permission.

6. THE GOSPEL ACCORDING TO JESUS, by John MacArthur Jr., 1988, 1993, 2008, Zondervan, Grand Rapids, MI 49530.

7. THE POPULAR ENCYCLOPEDIA OF BIBLE PROPHECY, by Tim LaHaye and Ed Hinson, 2004, Harvest House Publishers, Eugene, OR 97402

8. The NLT PROMISE BOOK FOR WOMEN, by Ronald A Beers, 2010, Tyndale House Pub.

9. Great Is Thy Faithfulness by Thomas O. Chisholm and William M. Runyan, 1923. Renewed, 1951, Hope Publishing Co., Carol Stream IL 60188. All rights reserved. Used by permission.

10. 25 MESSIANIC SIGNS IN ISRAEL TODAY by Noah Hutchings and GillaTreibich

A very important prayer to sing:

DURING YOUR QUIET TIME, YOUR PRAISE TIME AT CHURCH, ON A PICNIC, AT A RALLY, IN THE SHOWER, WHILE HIKING, AT YOUR MOTHER-IN-LAWS, WHEN YOU FEEL JOYFUL,. WHEN YOU ARE DEPRESSED...ANYTIME YOU WANT AN EXTRA SHOT OF FUEL FROM THE HOLY SPIRIT...(with your arms raised to Jesus and your fingers making like rain coming down, ending hands together at your heart...repeating the same movement every time you sing, "Rain down Your mercy on me.")

RAIN DOWN YOUR MERCY ON ME...

RAIN DOWN YOUR MERCY ON ME...

LORD, I SURRENDER,

IN THIS VERY HOUR...

RAIN DOWN YOUR MERCY ON ME!

(When you sing, "Lord, I surrender..." make an L with your right hand on your left shoulder, then on your right hip...then raise both hands open palms up, toward Him when you sing, "in this very hour...' next, come down with fingers trickling, Rain down your mercy on me," ending with both hands clasped over your heart...where the Holy Spirit is residing...POWERFUL! He will fill you with such love, you will be exploding with a feeling so breathtaking as to prove that old saying, "bursting at the seams!")

You'll want to run out into the street and holler:

"SEE WHAT HE HAS DONE FOR ME...HE HAS CLEANED ME UP AND MADE ME WHOLE!"

There is no way you can sing this song without coming into His presence!

He will honor this heartfelt prayer ANYTIME and ALL THE TIME because He loves you and wants you to be His—body and soul!

"Rain Down Your Mercy on Me," words and music by Joel Shoemake and Michelle Brazeal. Used with permission.